SWIMMING WITH ALEX BAUMANN

A PROGRAM FOR COMPETITIVE AND RECREATIONAL SWIMMERS

JENO TIHANYI & ALEX BAUMANN

KEY PORTER BOOKS

This book is dedicated to all the swimmers who seek excellence, to be the best they can be in fulfilling their dreams. This book is also dedicated to the parents who must make many personal sacrifices in helping to fulfill the dream of their children.

Last but not least, I dedicate this book to my family, Cathy, Miklos, Sacha, Andrey for the many years of unselfish support and unfulfilled promises.

— J.T.

Canadian Cataloguing in Publication Data

Tihanyi, Jeno
  Swimming with Alex Baumann

ISBN 1-55013-109-5

1. Swimming. I. Baumann, Alex. II. Title.

GV837.B38 1988   797.2'1   C88-095405-1

Key Porter Books Limited
70 The Esplanade
Toronto, Ontario
M5E 1R2

**Written in collaboration with
Sarah Silberstein Swartz.**

Special thanks to the management and staff
of the Etobicoke Olympium.

Illustrations: Dean Kalmantis
Typesetting: Compeer Typographic Services Limited

Printed and bound in Canada

89 90 91 92 93 6 5 4 3 2 1

CONTENTS

ACKNOWLEDGMENTS

A book such as this is the result of the collection of many ideas, experiences and research results, personal and borrowed.

Inspirational indebtedness has many sources. First and foremost, I am indebted to Alex "Sasa" Baumann, double gold medalist Olympian and world record holder and the best individual medley swimmer in the history of Canadian swimming. During his 14 years of swimming with me, Sasa helped me learn that the day-to-day seeking of excellence is the best nourishment to success.

Secondly, I am indebted to a number of sport scientists, such as Dr. Ken Sidney and co-worker Ron Lowrey for certain ideas that I adopted from their book on orienteering; Dr. Michael Houston for his information on nutrition; Drs. F.I. Katch and W.D. McArdle for using some direction from their book on nutrition and exercise; Dr. J.E. Counsilman for the many years of friendship and encouragement I received.

Thirdly, I am indebted to Howard Firby, the Dean of the Canadian swimming community, for all the many ideas and innovations he introduced into swimming and shared over the years. To Professor Jack Pomfret who was instrumental in the beginning of my coaching involvement. To all my coaches—the many swimmers in my programs who taught me well.

PREFACE

This book is written for all those who are interested in swimming, from the beginner to the serious competitor. The intention in writing this book was to outline the skills and training concepts used in developing Alex Baumann's talent, especially during his early years as a competitive swimmer.

Developing into a serious and successful competitive swimmer is like growing up: it takes time. Your early years in swimming should be spent establishing the best possible stroke skills and continually adjusting these skills as the body grows and changes. The dominant theme of every swimming session should be "not how fast, but how well" the skills are performed.

This book is meant for the enjoyment of the beginner or recreational swimmer, as well as the serious competitive swimmer. If you are a recreational swimmer, you will enjoy swimming much more if your skills are good and if you are able to swim for several minutes without stopping. Learning good stroke skills and developing basic endurance for your muscles and heart will be a satisfying and healthy experience. You might even find that you will become a pretty good swimmer, and may want to join your friends in a swim club.

It is not possible to write a book that tells you exactly how to reach the peak of your potential. But this book can assist you, the swimmer, in visualizing all the steps necessary in reaching that goal. This book is based on 14 years of actual contact work that produced the best swimmer Canada ever had. It presents a realistic and easy-to-learn collection of skills and training methods, as well as other important skill information.

Success comes to those who work not only hard, but also intelligently. Please read on and good luck in your pursuit of excellence.

JENO TIHANYI, PH.D.

ALEX BAUMANN ON SWIMMING

Every serious athlete longs for the opportunity to participate in the excitement and glamour of the Olympics. Athletes from over 100 countries participate in this, the world's largest athletic competition. Ever since swimming became a regular event at the Summer Olympic Games in 1896, talented participants from all over the world have competed for the title of the fastest swimmer in their specialty. Up until 1984, no one from Canada had won gold medals in swimming since 1912, when George Hodgson of Montreal struck gold in two events.

Winning my two gold medals at the 1984 Olympics in Los Angeles was like a dream come true. I remember thinking, as I stood on the podium to accept my second gold medal, that this would certainly be the pinnacle of my swimming career. Not only was I part of the Canadian National Swimming Team competing in the Olympics, but I was also being recognized as the fastest individual medley swimmer in the world. It was a proud and unforgettable moment for me when the Canadian national anthem was played and a crowd of people from all over the world cheered and applauded.

It seemed like a dream at the time, but my gold medals were the result of 14 years of tough and uncompromising training. Swimming has been my lifelong obsession. For years, I followed a gruelling schedule of five to six hours of workouts a day, six days a week, 340 days a year. I had time for little else. Sometimes, I swam as much as 16 kilometres in one day. I knew what it meant to follow the rules of strenuous training, to go to bed at 9:30 every night so I could follow a blue line in the water at 5:30 in the morning. Before an especially important competition, I sometimes did nothing but sleep, eat and swim. I had sacrificed my social life — as a teenager, when it means the most — and sometimes even my studies, in order to devote myself to the sport of competitive swimming.

It wasn't always like this. As a small child, I loved the water, as most kids do, but I didn't want to work at swimming. I was more interested in splashing around and having a good time, than in learning the strokes. Though my mother had been a successful competitive swimmer in Czechoslovakia in the 1940s, she didn't teach me to swim until I was five years old. I think she was probably wise in not pushing me at an early age. She let me just enjoy the water.

And enjoy the water I did. During my early childhood, we lived near the ocean in Christchurch, New Zealand, and I spent as much time in the water as I could. I remember jumping the waves

Victory salute at the 1984 Summer Olympic Games.
LAZI PERENYI

Showing the strain of competition as a 10-year-old.

JOSH GOLDHAR

and playing water games with other kids. I am sure that I discovered my joy in swimming at this time—the exhilaration of being in the water, of stretching and moving under water, of feeling weightless.

I think most children are attracted to water. It's important to build on their natural interest in waterplay and help them gain confidence in the water, while they are still young and having fun. Whether you become interested in competitive swimming or swim for fitness and recreation, your first experience with water has a great deal to do with your later confidence in swimming. Pushing children too hard at too early an age is just as bad as overprotecting them and never allowing them near the water.

JOINING A TEAM: THE NOVICE SWIMMER

It is hard, if not impossible, to train alone. There is just too little motivation to swim lengths in a pool, back and forth, all by yourself. So much of the inspiration and encouragement in swimming comes from the team experience. This is why most young swimmers who are interested in training join a club, become part of a team and work with a coach.

After we moved to Canada in 1969, I was ready for more of a challenge. My older brother joined the Laurentian University Swim Club in Sudbury, Ontario, when it first started in 1973. I had always been influenced by my big brother, so I wanted to join too. My parents were concerned about my starting training too early, but when I turned nine, they relented and enrolled me in the club that was to change my life.

I was very excited about my first day at LUSC. I went with my brother, who was 16 at the time, and soon discovered that I would have to train with his group for the day because no younger groups were training. I was, of course, the youngest, slowest and least experienced swimmer there and I was repeatedly lapped. This might have discouraged me, but I was motivated by the fact that I was swimming with the best swimmers in the club. My experience that day foreshadowed my future.

At the age of nine, I regarded swimming as more of a social event than a competitive sport. The pool can be a very social environment. You talk between sets, you work out together, you crack a few jokes, you swim a few races and you try to beat one another without too much pressure. Our coach, Dr. Jeno Tihanyi, whom we called "Doc", knew that pre-teens have a very limited attention span. He kept us interested by adding friendly competitions, such as relay races and water polo, to our practical drills.

When we first started training, we novice swimmers were all in the same boat. There was a strong sense of camaraderie and equality at the club. None of us knew how to swim very well and we all had a lot to learn. We all began with the same one-hour workouts, three times a week. These workouts were the same for everyone in our group and few swimmers got individual attention. In this atmosphere, many friendships and some healthy rivalries developed.

Thank goodness for this friendly atmosphere, because swim training soon became very tough. Dr. Tihanyi pushed us to work very hard and tried to get us to perform to our full potential. Sometimes I resented his disciplinary ways, but mostly I respected his determination to make us into the finest swimmers we were capable of becoming.

When it came to technique, Doc was a stickler. Technique is one of the most important aspects of swimming. Without good technique, you can't swim efficiently, no matter how much you practise. When I first joined the club, my stroke technique was not very good. Doc taught me about efficient swimming — how not to expend more energy than you need, and how to move smoothly and fast. We worked on various skills and on strengthening exercises to offset my weak points. Gradually my strokes began to improve. Even today I may not have perfect strokes, but I have a very efficient push and pull under water, thanks to years of work with Doc.

I was also influenced by Dr. Tihanyi's emphasis on realistic goals. I never set out with the conscious goal of competing in the Olympics. Instead, Doc and I set very small goals, right from the beginning. Once I mastered one goal, I would move on to the next. I was always very realistic in setting goals within my capabilities and it always gave me a great sense of accomplishment to rise to the next level. In this way, I climbed the competitive ladder until finally I reached the Olympics.

After a year of training at the club, it became apparent that I was excelling in my group. Though Doc did not give me any special treatment, he began to build up my training until, by the age of 10, I was training as much as four hours a day.

Because my times were now quite fast, I was put into Level I, the leading group. My peers were now five or six years older than me and much faster. It was a real challenge to keep up with them. But then, I always enjoyed having someone faster than me in the next lane: it spurred me to train harder.

The camaraderie is an essential facet of swimming with a team.

JOSH GOLDHAR

Climax of a successful swim meet in London, Ontario, in 1974.

JOSH GOLDHAR

COMPETITION: THE ADVANCED SWIMMER

Although it was apparent at an early age that I had a talent for swimming, I was also very self-motivated. It wasn't so much that Dr. Tihanyi worked me harder than the others, but that I pushed

Watching the competition from the side of the pool when I was 10.

JOSH GOLDHAR

myself. I knew I wanted to succeed and I was prepared to work for it. Sometimes Doc had to take me out of the pool and tell me not to overdo it.

I didn't always enjoy training. Often, it was the camaraderie and the thrill of competition that kept me going. There is a lot of competition in training; it doesn't just happen at meets. You're always pushing one another to make progress and better your times. It's an important form of competition, and it's learned pretty early in the game.

I wasn't competitive when I started, but when I saw other people winning races, I thought: I want to do that. During my first competitive race in Sudbury at the age of nine, I was disqualified—I touched the finishing wall with only one hand during the breaststroke. But after the next meet, I came in third twice in a row and I suddenly wanted to beat the swimmers who had beaten me. I knew that the only way I could do this was by training harder. I made it my goal to beat these competitors. Within a couple of months I succeeded.

Sometimes the best motivation is pride. I remember, when I was 11, another swimmer laughed at me because, although I had won a race, I had missed the national age group record by one-hundredth of a second. Later, I raced against this swimmer in his specialty, the 100-metre butterfly. His laughter had made me so angry that I put all my energy into beating him. I won that race by that same one-hundredth of a second. It was my revenge and it gave me great satisfaction.

When I was 13, I started training for the individual medley (IM), which became my specialty. I don't think I so much chose it, as it was chosen for me because I was so efficient at it. Because of my extensive training, I had learned the skills and was very competent in all four strokes. My best stroke was the breaststroke and I had set my first national record in the backstroke at the age of nine. I didn't really have a weak stroke. This made me a perfect IM swimmer, since IM combines all four strokes. From the time Doc discovered I was good at it, I trained and competed mostly in the IM event.

There is nothing like the excitement of going to meets. You start off with the regional meets among 12 to 15 clubs in your area. If you're good enough to qualify, you move on to the provincial championships which take place two or three times a year. From there, it's on to the national championships, where the top two swimmers from each event make up the Canadian National Swimming Team. This team represents Canada at various international meets, including the World Championships and the Olympics.

I won my first national championship in 1978, at the age of 14, but it was really my first international experience in Florida, at the age of 11, that made the biggest impression on me. It was my first meet outside Canada and the first time I competed against non-Canadian swimmers. This competition was very significant in my development because it gave me different rewards: the chance to travel and make new friends. I discovered that I loved to travel and it became a definite incentive to be able to compete in another country.

People often say that competitive swimmers miss so much, both socially and in their formal education, because of their heavy training schedule. But I feel I've learned much more because of my swimming. I've learned discipline and the rewards of hard work. I've travelled all over the world in the past 14 years and that's been an education in itself. I've also met a lot of interesting people along the way, many of whom have become my close friends. In fact, I first met my wife Tracy at the 1982 Commonwealth Games in Australia.

I've learned how to cope with both winning and losing. Competition has taught me how to set realistic goals and how to pursue something I really want. Swimming has also helped me to organize my life. Because of my intensive training schedule, I had to get things done in a limited amount of time. In fact, when I didn't swim I got worse marks in school than when I was in training, probably because there were fewer limitations on my time. When I was swimming, I knew I had two specific hours each day that were set aside for studying.

In 1980, I was chosen for the ultimate competition—the Olympics. But because the Moscow Olympics were boycotted, our

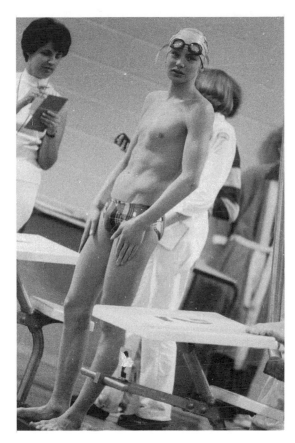

A backstroke event.

JOSH GOLDHAR

Sharing a joke after the finish of a race at an age-group meet in Ottawa.

JOSH GOLDHAR

Discussing strategy at the Nationals in Montreal, 1981.

ATHLETE INFORMATION BUREAU

Canadian team didn't go. It was unfortunate, but, for me, perhaps it was just as well. It might have been a good learning experience, but I wasn't at the peak of my ability. I might have won a medal, but I certainly wasn't ready for gold. It was a tragedy, however, for those athletes who had been training for years and for whom there would never be another chance.

For me, it all started to come together four years later at the June 1984 Olympic trials. In preparing for the trials, I was training five to six hours and swimming up to 15 kilometres a day. I had previously broken the 200-metre IM world record twice, once in 1981 in Heidelberg, West Germany, and again the next year at the Commonwealth Games in Brisbane, Australia. There was a lot of pressure on me, especially from my fellow Canadians, because I was expected to win at the Olympics. The trials were critical because I was afraid of not qualifying for the Olympic team. As things turned out, I not only made the team, but I also broke the 400-metre IM world record. From there, I went on to the Los Angeles Olympics, to better my own records and win two Olympic gold medals.

THE MAKING OF AN OLYMPIC CHAMPION

People often ask me what it takes to be a great swimmer. I believe there's a fine line between being good and being a champion. Above all, you've got to be totally committed to your sport in order to achieve greatness. My own dedication was based on my love of swimming, my desire to win and my need to accomplish certain personal goals. From the time I was 10 years old, I woke up at 5:00 each morning eager to work hard at the pool. That attitude never changed.

For a long time, I didn't consider myself to be a great swimmer. I remember thinking, at an age-group meet in 1974, that I had the potential to be good, but I didn't know whether I was championship material. In fact, I didn't realize that I was very good until I reached the international senior level in 1978, and even then I didn't think of myself as great. It wasn't until I broke my first world record in 1981 that the reality of my true potential began to sink in.

It was lucky that I had the ideal swimmer's body: tall and lean, with a long back and long muscles. But you can always work to improve your physical attributes. If I hadn't been a swimmer and lifted weights as part of my training, I'm sure I would have been quite a scrawny guy. The Brazilian, Ricardo Prado, who came in behind me in the 1984 Olympics, was only five feet six. So obviously, you can overcome many physical disadvantages with dedicated training.

Talent is perhaps 50 per cent of what makes a great swimmer. In my case, the fact that my mother was a successful swimmer, my father was athletic and my brother made the national swim team says something about my inherited talent. But you can't make it on talent alone. You must enjoy the sport and have a driving desire to train and compete. Without this desire, the training and sheer hard work, I would never have made it to the top.

The drive for personal excellence and self-improvement is essential. Winning is not always the most important thing; doing your best is. For example, after I won my gold medals, the pressure to better myself was enormous. I was considered the fastest swimmer in the world in my event, and for a while I had little competition other than my own world records. During the 1986 World Championships in Madrid, I was unexpectedly weakened by a severe case of the flu. I knew that if I competed I would probably lose, but I needed to get in there and do my best. I didn't win, but I did manage a bronze and a silver medal. I was pleased with my performance in those races because I felt that I had done my best under the circumstances.

In our society, there is too much emphasis on winning. Young swimmers, especially, often attach too little importance to self-improvement and attaining their own personal best. That's where the coach comes in. A good coach knows how to get 100 per cent out of his or her swimmers. The coach can also gauge the actual and potential abilities of individual swimmers. By encouraging young swimmers to strive toward realistic goals, he or she can make winning become less important. Improving next time is what counts.

Self-improvement requires constructive self-criticism. Self-assessment should be practical and positive, so that it doesn't undermine confidence. There is no such thing as a perfect race and you can always improve. Even in the excitement of my first world record in 1981, my coach and I looked at the race to see what I did incorrectly. We knew that with the 1984 Olympics there were tough challenges ahead.

My Olympic performances were the closest to perfection that I've ever come, but I still feel that there were some parts that could have been improved. I watched a tape of my Olympic 200-metre race and at first I didn't think I could have done any better. But after seeing the tape five or six times, I began to notice opportunities for improvement. For example, one of my turns wasn't as fast as it could have been. I would never put down my performance at the Olympics. I'm very proud of it and I know I did my best. But it is important to look at yourself critically and to see areas where you can improve.

Good swimming strategy is also very important in the making of a champion, especially the individual medley swimmer. For example, it is important to know the strengths and weaknesses of

At the end of a race, I check the scoreboard for my time.

ATHLETE INFORMATION BUREAU

At the 1984 Olympic Trials in Montreal: a good athlete-coach relationship was fundamental to my success as a swimmer.

JOSH GOLDHAR

your competition and act accordingly. Most swimmers have at least one weak stroke. If you can gain on that, you have a greater chance of winning. Conversely, if you're competing against a fast butterfly swimmer in the first length of the individual medley, for example, you know he's going to go fast at the outset. So it won't scare you if he's a body length ahead of you. You can always catch up at the end, when it counts.

Visualization has been an important element in my strategy. Doc taught me to imagine the race beforehand in order to prepare myself for it. I would see myself at every stage of the race: the start, the turns and the finish. We would always establish goal times and split up the race into the four strokes, called "splits", to make my visualization more accurate and more realistic. I knew I was capable of doing each split well and sometimes these four splits would add up to a new world record.

Over the years, I've become better at visualization. I know exactly what I want to do and where I want to be at certain parts of the race. About a half hour before a race, I find a quiet spot and start visualizing the race in my mind. Ten minutes before the race, I stop this exercise. Visualization must be timed so that you don't become overstimulated just before the race. If you go out too fast, you can easily lose.

All great athletes have had to overcome their share of personal setbacks on their road to success. For me, it was a chronic shoulder problem. I first began to notice it in April, 1981. It started as a very gradual pain in my right shoulder, which got worse and worse. I later found out I had a condition called subluxation, which is usually the result of overuse and too much flexibility in a joint.

I kept swimming, but I couldn't escape the pain. Finally, I took a couple of weeks off, but this didn't help at all. So I decided to start training again despite the pain, in order to make it to a competition against the German and Soviet teams in Heidelberg, West Germany. Of course, I had to pull back in my training because of my injury and concentrate on sprints rather than long distances. In the end, I not only made it to the competition, but I also broke my first world record in the 200-metre IM.

Later that year, I went to Indiana University to train with another well-known coach, Dr. James Counsilman. I couldn't swim. The pain in my shoulder had become so excruciating that I couldn't even sleep. I went from doctor to doctor looking for help. Some doctors suggested exercise to strengthen the joint; others suggested total rest. Still others told me I needed surgery. I became very confused and frustrated. Most worrisome of all, several doctors told me that my competitive swimming career was over. It was a terrible year for me.

I decided to go back to Sudbury in January 1982, because I needed the comfort of familiar surroundings. When I returned to the Laurentian University Swim Club, Dr. Tihanyi was a great help. With his support and the medical advice of orthopedic surgeon Dr. Peter Fowler of London, Ontario, I started a rehabilitation program and began to recover. I still had a lot of pain, but with weight training and slow exercises, my shoulder was soon much better.

In October 1982, I decided I was ready for the Commonwealth Games in Brisbane, Australia. Psychologically, it was very hard for me to re-enter competition. After having broken a world record in 1981, I had been out of action for about a year. I wondered whether I would ever be on top again. But I pulled myself together and managed to set my second world record at the Commonwealth Games. This world record meant even more to me than the first. Nothing fazed me after this, because I had been through a period when I thought my career was over, and survived it. I was now reassured that I could go on to even greater achievements.

In sports, and in life, there will always be obstacles to achievement. If you can adjust to your setbacks, learn from them and not let them destroy you, you will become both a better competitor and a better person.

Part of preparing for a race is imagining how it will be—visualization.

ATHLETE INFORMATION BUREAU

Signing autographs at the Olympic Trials in 1984.

JOSH GOLDHAR

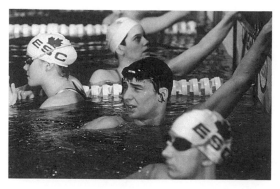

Near the end of my career as a competitive swimmer:
Toronto, 1986.

ATHLETE INFORMATION BUREAU

In competition in Vancouver in 1985. After the Los
Angeles Olympics it was hard to maintain my competitive desire.

ATHLETE INFORMATION BUREAU

LOOKING BACK

People consider age 20 to be the brink of adulthood. It is, usually, a time for beginnings. Most 20-year-olds are just starting out on a career, a family of their own or a higher education.

I was 20 years old when I won my gold medals. By that time, I was already at the peak of my swimming career and had been training and competing for 11 years. I wasn't very old, really, but as a swimmer I was getting close to retirement.

Swimming is a young people's sport. It is one of the most stren-uous forms of athletic competition. It entails continuous training from an early age, many hours of practice in the pool every day, a great deal of mental concentration—and a lot of pressure. There is a limit to the number of years you can push yourself to perform at this level.

The time of greatest competitive potential, the "peak", is in the late teens for women, from the early to mid twenties for men. Few swimmers stay in competitive swimming past this peak. Some start training so early and are pushed so hard that they burn out. They are compelled to retire because of the stress inflicted on both body and mind. Because I was such a precocious swimmer I was expected to burn out early. In fact, by the time I retired, I had competed for 14 years.

The recognition and publicity that came with the Olympic gold medals I won in 1984 changed my life. But when the cheering died down and I returned home, the question I faced was: what would I do for an encore? I knew I still had a couple of years of swimming left in me, but I faced a tough decision: should I con-tinue training so hard—and for what purpose?

I still had the desire to win, but all future competitions paled by comparison to the Los Angeles Games. Very few people who have won gold return to another Olympic competition. It's just too anticlimactic. After the Games, I also found there was no one to compete against. It would be another three years before other swimmers would challenge my world records. In the circumstan-ces, my only incentive for continued competition was to beat my own world records, and this was not sufficient. My desire to train and compete was waning.

In 1987, I realized I had accomplished everything I wanted to. It was time to move on to other things. I no longer wanted to put the rest of my life on hold. I retired from competition.

Since the Olympics, I've undergone a kind of detraining. I still swim at the club three times a week. I do weight training and I still race against the clock. Sometimes I race against young, up-and-coming swimmers. Maybe I shouldn't be as competitive as I am, but it takes a long time to break an old habit.

My experience as a CBC sports commentator for the swimming events of the 1988 Olympic Games in Seoul was insightful and reassuring for me personally. It was very strange to be on the other side, watching rather than competing. But after observing the first race, I knew that I had made the right choice by retiring when I did. I remembered well the enormous pressures the athletes were under and I recognized the work and commitment required to get to the Olympic level. In Seoul, I had to admit that I was relieved not to have to put in the time and energy necessary to maintain my world ranking. It was a pleasure just to sit back and watch the excitement.

Today, I am very proud of my achievements, but I like to let them speak for themselves. Gold medals are merely one symbol of success. For me, success is also measured by my own sense of personal accomplishment. Breaking six world records and establishing 11 world best standards was gratifying. That I worked so hard for so long to reach the top of my sport made the experience all the more rewarding.

Looking back, I'm glad I had my swimming career, with all its triumphs, as well as its hard work and sacrifices. I owe so much to the sport of swimming. I just hope I've left a good example for young swimmers of the future to follow—one that will inspire you to pursue your goals and realize your highest dreams.

Receiving the gold medal at the World University Games in Edmonton, in 1983.

DAVE STUBBS

Part II is the technical basis of the Alex Baumann Swimming Program. It is the methodical and scientific training system which helped Alex win his Olympic gold medals.

This technical section is divided into segments devoted to the four strokes commonly used in competitive swimming. The strokes are followed by a segment on the individual medley, Alex's gold medal specialty, which combines all four strokes in one exciting event.

The individual medley is placed at the end of the technical section, because it is the culmination of all four strokes. The individual medley should be added to the learning process as soon as the skills for at least two strokes have been learned reasonably well. Since the freestyle and the breaststroke are learned first and are the end strokes in the individual medley, it is easy to combine them. However, serious training for the individual medley should not begin until you have mastered all four strokes.

The four swim strokes discussed in this book are used in competitive swimming because they are the fastest, most efficient ways to swim. Whether you are a recreational swimmer or a competitive swimmer, you can use the instructions and drills described in this book to learn the skills and the best technique for each of the strokes. The main difference between swimming the strokes in competition and swimming them for recreation or fitness is not in the technique, but in the speed of the arm and leg movements. The strokes remain the same. Another difference is that in recreational swimming it is not necessary to follow the strict rules of competition. These rules are used to keep competitors' actions standardized during a race, so that no swimmer has an unfair advantage over the others.

The order of the strokes in this book — freestyle, breaststroke, backstroke and butterfly — indicate a natural progression in learning. Traditionally, most people in North America learn the freestyle first. It is most like the natural walking and running skill patterns of children, and therefore the easiest to learn. People also seem to have a natural aptitude for learning the breaststroke. By the time a swimmer is comfortable with the freestyle and the breaststroke, learning the backstroke and the butterfly should come naturally and easily.

Do remember that although you should concentrate first on the freestyle, then the breaststroke, and so on, no stroke should be learned in isolation. Many of the fundamental skills are common to all strokes. Therefore the basic skills are teaching elements of all the strokes. It is strongly recommended that the leg action

Resting between drills.

MARCO CHIESA

of all four strokes be learned along with elementary stroke drills in freestyle, breaststroke, and so on.

As a serious swimmer it is important for you to have a clear understanding of every aspect of each stroke, no matter how small. You will notice in this book that "The Technique" section for each stroke is divided into "Body position", "Leg action", "Arm action", "Breathing", "The start" and "The turn". These sub-sections are organised in the order the skills should be learned. However, the skills you learn for each stroke are cumulative and it is therefore important to combine, for example, the kicking of the leg action with what you have already learned about the body position.

Just as the strokes are divided into different actions, each arm action is further broken into smaller phases, such as "The recovery phase" and "The entry phase". By separating each phase when you swim, you will find them easier to remember. If you learn the action phases separately, you will also be able to make corrections more easily when your coach is pointing out incorrect technique.

It is good practice to think of one aspect of the skill you are learning at a time, rather than trying to remember everything at once. For example, for half a pool length, you might think of your kicking. For the next length, concentrate on your recovery, then combine the two. Next work on your entry, and so on.

The "Drills" that follow each section are organized in order of difficulty and you should follow that order. You are welcome to choose to spend less time on some and more time on others. But it is important that you do not skip drills, even if they appear to be easy. Never rush the drills and do go back to them from time to time.

"Objectives for the stroke" appear at the beginning of each new stroke and provide a short summary of the simple but important technical goals to be remembered when you practise the stroke. "Learning tips", the "dos" and "don'ts" for each skill, reinforce important suggestions that are indispensable for your learning. "Points to remember" highlight the key skill concepts for that section.

The "Learning progressions" are sections to remind you of the logical order in which to learn your skills. Just as you would not start to build the roof of a house before the foundation, you need to start with the basic skills—the foundation upon which you can build.

This book emphasizes the scientific skill learning approach to competitive swimming, with the growing and developing young athlete in mind. From the very first time that Alex started training with me, the emphasis was always on skills and technique, rather than on speed. Our approach to swimming was always based on the credo, "not how fast, but how well".

Striving for excellence has always been central to Alex's success. At every training session and every swim meet, Alex tried to swim more efficiently and improve one or two skills to perfection. Over the years, this skill learning approach to swimming helped him master good technique and the most minute aspects of each stroke. It was his hard work, his dedication to swimming and his strong commitment to my swimming program that developed Alex Baumann into an Olympic gold winner and a world record holder in his sport.

On the podium after accepting the gold medal for victory in the 200-metre Individual Medley at the Los Angeles Summer Olympic Games.

ATHLETE INFORMATION BUREAU

1. THE FREESTYLE

Alex talks about the freestyle

When I started competitive swimming at the age of nine, freestyle was the first stroke I learned. Being the fastest and easiest of strokes to perform, it soon became a favourite of mine. It feels exhilarating to be able to move fast through the water, and the better my technique became, the faster I could swim. Later my inherent competitiveness made me enjoy the stroke even more, particularly when I began to win races.

As do all young swimmers starting out, I had many problems to correct with my freestyle. One of the biggest problems I had was that I tended to over-rotate on the recovery which caused my whole body to turn on its side and slow me down.

It was also a challenge learning flip turns. In an attempt to have a fast turn, I would flip my legs over straight, which would cause my body to go too deep. It should have been a tucked and shallow turn. I continued to do my turns the wrong way until one day, during a race in a particularly shallow pool, I almost hit my head on the bottom. I quickly realized what I was doing wrong and worked hard to correct my flip turns.

As with all sports, practice is very important. And, of course, repeating the correct technique is the goal. If you repeat poor technique, it will only reinforce the errors. That is why it is important for young swimmers to do stroke drills. These drills are designed to "force" the swimmers to perform the correct technique and make them notice where the mistakes are.

Catch up (one arm after another, each hand touching after the recovery), one-arm freestyle, and bilateral breathing drills are all effective in helping the swimmer maintain a stable body position, preventing over-rotation, and getting maximum speed and glide from the stroke.

Doc explains all these drills in this section. I hope you find them as helpful as I did when I was learning.

FACTS ABOUT THE FREESTYLE

The freestyle stroke is the fastest competitive stroke. It combines a flutter kick with an alternating over-the-water arm stroke and rhythmic breathing.

In freestyle competition, swimmers can use any stroke they wish. Since the front crawl is the fastest stroke, it is the one most often used, and has therefore come to mean the same thing as the freestyle stroke. Although swimmers sometimes swim other strokes during freestyle for the sake of practice, in competition the time is always officially recorded as front crawl.

The *front crawl* is the stroke that most closely resembles the instinctive movements of a baby learning to move by crawling. Even a non-swimmer's dog paddle is a variation of this crawling action. New swimmers often begin with this stroke because it is

Freestyle—the fastest stroke.

MARCO CHIESA

the most natural movement in the water and therefore easiest to learn.

The background
The freestyle stroke has gone through several changes. At first, it resembled the dog paddle, then the sidestroke. Next it became a modified sidestroke with one arm recovering over the water. Later came the Australian crawl, introduced by an Australian swimmer in 1900. The straight-legged kicking action associated with the Australian crawl later evolved into the present flutter kick.

Today the stroke is performed with many variations, all of which are within the rules. This is why it has become known as the freestyle.

Freestyle swimming appeared at the first modern Olympic Games in 1896.

The action
The freestyle combines the flutter kick—the rapid up and down movement of the feet—and the alternating over-the-water recovery of the arms. Most swimmers develop a rhythm that allows three kicks for every completed arm cycle. In the middle of this rhythmic action, the swimmer takes one breath.

Good freestyle technique minimizes the force of the water against your body, called water resistance or *drag*. A stretched-out horizontal body position and economical kicking action will keep your body elevated and in good balance. Your arm strokes should be smooth and evenly timed. Your breathing should also be even and must not interfere with your swimming. Through drills and regular practice, you can learn to keep your body stretched out and high in the water to help your kicking and the roll of your body. Use your arms to power you through the water.

Objectives for the freestyle stroke

- Keep the up-and-down movement of the legs continuous and loose.
- Allow your body to float high.
- Maintain continuity in the stroke by making sure that one arm is always working in the water.
- Roll the body in one streamlined unit, especially when you are taking a breath.

THE TECHNIQUE

Body position
You will never be able to get rid of the water resistance that slows you down, but proper body position can reduce it. Stretch out in the water so the water can support you.

The ability of the body to float in water is called its *buoyancy*.

The force of the water pressure, which determines your buoyancy, is the difference between the weight of the water that your body displaces and the weight of your body. The body will float when its weight is less than the water it displaces. The body will sink when its weight is more.

Some people float better than others. Floating ability is influenced by three factors: body position, lung capacity and body type. Your body is mainly made up of muscle, bone and fat. Fat floats, while bone and muscle sink. Therefore muscular and bony people are poor floaters. Body composition has nothing to do with whether a person can swim or not. Those swimmers who are poor floaters must learn to kick efficiently to compensate for their deficiency. It is important to have a stretched-out body position that distributes the body weight well, regardless of your body type.

Fig. 1.1.   Basic freestyle body position. Note sloping body from head to feet.

Learning tip
To make sure you stay as horizontal as possible, look at an imaginary floating object just out of reach of your out-stretched arm. That object will be the base of your thumb as your hand enters the water. The important point to remember is to constantly look forward, in order to keep yourself horizontal.

The trunk position

Your trunk, the torso of your body, is the biggest floating surface of your body. It serves the same purpose as a boat bottom. The bottom of the boat provides a large surface area, with evenly distributed weight, that helps the boat to be stable and float well. The trunk of your body has the same potential. When it is well extended, it keeps the body in good balance and enhances your floating ability.

The level of your shoulders depends on the distance you will be covering. For longer distances, your body will be more submerged than it is when you swim sprints. In either position, you will feel the water's buoyant support of your torso. This elevation will make sure you stay in the required horizontal position. Your body will also slope down slightly from your shoulders to your feet, so your legs will remain in the water and work efficiently.

Learning tip
To ensure a well elevated and properly positioned trunk, be sure to keep your chin forward and just below the level of the water.

The head position

Hold your head as you do when you walk, with your chin tilted slightly forward. The waterline will be between your eyebrows

a

b

Fig. 1.2. Freestyle body position drill on the pool deck. Note streamlined body shape.

and your hairline. From this position, you can see the bottom of the pool at the same time that you look forward. When you assume this head position, the natural rolling action of your body will make it easy for you to breathe. The rest of your body will slope down slightly toward your feet.

Keep your eyes open! You need to check your body position and the visible parts of your stroke. You also need to keep track of the other swimmers in a race and be aware of your coach's instructions during training.

The leg position

Your legs perform an important part of the freestyle stroke. But if you do not use your legs the right way, they can destroy the effectiveness of your body position. Remember that your legs should never be spread wider than the width of your body or they will create the drag that you are working to cut down. When you practise, picture yourself swimming through a 50 cm pipe and then through a 40 cm pipe without changing the way you do your stroke. The legs should always be the deepest part of the body position.

Learning tip

Imagine that your body is sloping from the head to your feet, as if your body was teeter-tottering. Make sure your feet remain under water and your shoulders skid at the surface. Your body should feel like a sailboard skidding on the surface with the rear keel under water controlling the board, just as your feet control your body.

Points to remember about the freestyle body position

- Always stretch forward well, with the eyes looking forward.
- Keep your shoulders higher than the rest of your body.
- Never allow your body to sway from side-to-side.

Drills

1. Practise proper body position on the pool deck to develop a feel for the position. Stack three kickboards on the deck and stretch out on top of them, face down. Assume a balanced position with your arms and legs extended straight out. Put your hands on top of each other and look at the base of your thumbs, making sure that your arms cover your ears. This is your basic *glide position*. When performed in the water, it is held as long as the body moves with correct body control. Hold this position for about 10 seconds and then relax. Repeat this several times. Hold your breath while doing this drill.

2. Practise *gliding* in the water to improve your control and distance. At first, push off and forward from the bottom of the pool with your arms extended, hands on top of each other (as in drill number 1). Allow your legs to rise to just below the surface, fully extended. Make sure your arms cover your ears and look at the base of your thumbs. Again, hold your breath.

   Glide until your legs begin to sink. After you have practised this several times, try it with your eyes closed. This will help you to feel the correct position.

3. Repeat the gliding practice, but this time push off from the end of the pool, under water, and hold the same body position. This drill will create greater speed than the previous one, so it will be easier to keep your body horizontal. It will also help you begin to practise the correct way to push away from the wall after a turn.

   Concentrate on assuming a comfortable but correct head position, one that allows you to see the bottom of the pool as well as to look forward. Practise until you can consistently

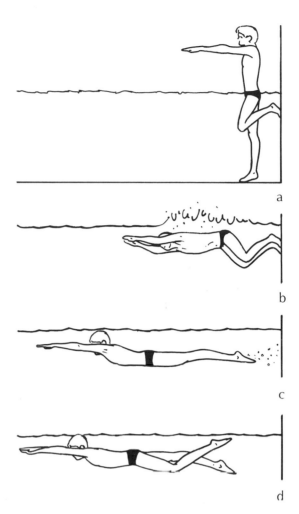

Fig. 1.3.   Front-glide with push-off from pool wall.

Fig. 1.4.   Prone glide freestyle kicking.

assume a correct head position that feels right. Your coach or a friend could help you with this drill by checking your head position.

Leg action

Now that you are comfortable with your head and body position, it's time to get your legs into action. The leg action is usually referred to as *kicking*, but the kicking should be a relaxed, supple, alternating movement of your legs. The movement should be like a long backward extension of your legs with your feet drifting down at the end, rather than a directly downward movement.

In freestyle, the movement of your legs holds your body in position and in balance. Your body will be sloping slightly downward from your shoulders to create a diagonal plane instead of a strictly horizontal one. This position helps the natural rolling action of your body. Your legs don't really give you any speed unless you're sprinting and are in a higher body position, like a hydroplane.

Your legs contribute to your speed at the start of a swim and during turns when you drive off the block or the wall of the pool. But if you are swimming any distance in freestyle, your legs should be working to keep your body in balance while it is rolling in the water. Your legs also maintain the flow of your motion and proper body position at the start, during turns and while sprinting.

The recovery phase

The kick recovery is really the preparation for the next kick, so it must be done accurately. To avoid bending your knee while your leg is moving back up, concentrate on lifting the back of your knee. This will again force your legs to move from your hip. As your leg moves up, relax and stretch your foot at the ankle. Stop moving your leg up when your heel breaks the surface. Flex your knee slightly and start your leg down again—from the hip. (See Figure 1.4, recovering leg.)

You will need to practise your kick every time you swim. Work at it until you can perform the correct movement without thinking about it. Since you cannot see your own leg action to check it yourself, have a friend or your coach or teacher watch your progress until you can feel what is correct.

The drive phase

In order to get the most out of your leg action, forget about bending your knees. The general rule is that the legs move at the hip joint, as if each leg were a long fin, rhythmically coiling and uncoiling. Your legs should stay relaxed so they will be supple. Your knees should flex slightly rather than bend. It is this flexing of the knee that starts the downward movement at your hip. It must be relaxed enough to allow the action to travel along the length of your leg, finishing like an uncoiling whip with a bang at the end.

While your legs are moving down, your feet will be stretched to allow your toes to trail behind and give you the whip at the end of the move. If any speed is created by your kicking, it will be by your feet, which serve as propellers.

To make your feet whip like flippers, position them with your toes turned inward as your leg moves down. Then rotate your foot to the vertical position as though you were *sculling*. Sculling is like the propeller action of a motorboat. As the feet rotate to change position, they grab fresh water resistance. This intoed position of your feet will provide some sculling as your feet go through the intoed-to-vertical-to-intoed positions. The concept of sculling is further explained in the section on "Arm Action", below.

Remember that the more flexible your ankle joints are, the more productive the final part of your kick will be. Also, remember that stiff ankles and kicking will often give you spasms in your foot and calf muscles. So float your legs through the kicking action, rather than driving them by force.

Learning tip
While kicking, keep your body long and stretched out, so your feet can follow a backward-and-downward path as well as downward.

Learning tip
Daily flexibility exercises are very important to develop supple ankle joints. Since your leg muscles are the largest muscles in your body, daily kicking routines should be practised to develop and maintain strength.

Points to remember about the freestyle leg action

- Always stretch out your legs. Keep them loose and supple with a slight bend at the knees.
- Keep your kicking legs under the water at all times.
- Always kick hard when approaching and leaving the wall.

Drills

1. Assume the correct horizontal body position and hold onto the lip of the pool with one hand. Place the other hand, fingers pointing down, on the pool wall for support. Take a deep breath, put your face in the water and alternately move your legs up and down. Kick slowly and review details of the movement. Concentrate on only one aspect of the kick at a time — hips, knees, foot action, recovery. Maintain the correct head position and body alignment, and learn to feel the loose float-

Fig. 1.5.   Freestyle kicking with kickboard.

ing action of your legs. Once you've established the action of the kick, speed it up gradually, until you can feel yourself trying to move the wall.

2. This is a repeat of the third body position drill, with an added leg action. Push off from the end of the pool under water into a *prone glide* (your body on the front), hands on top of each other. (See Figure 1.3.) Look at the base of your thumbs and kick for as long as you can in one breath. This will allow you to practise the extended body position that keeps your body floating high. Concentrate on the skill rather than trying to kick for a long distance. Does it feel right? Are your feet sculling properly?

   As a variation on this drill, begin under water as you would after a turn. Kicking under water will give you a feel for how well the water pressure is distributed over your body. It will also give you practice pushing off the wall as you should after a turn, develop your kick and help your breath control. Repeat.

3. In this drill, you will cover a longer distance, so use a kickboard. To make sure that it doesn't interfere with the mechanics you have practised so far, learn the correct way to hold the board: at arm's length, both arms resting on the board and your hands over the front edge. In this position, your shoulders will be level with the surface, your face will be in the water and your eyes can be fixed on the end of the board instead of the base of your thumbs. Kick for 50 metres and rest for about 30 seconds. Repeat the drill six to 10 times.

   If you want to increase the difficulty of this drill, try a higher head position that raises your shoulders out of the water. You will have to kick much harder to keep your legs near the surface. This will build the strength you need to be successful in sprinting.

   Always follow up this drill with kicking without the board, especially if you are going to continue practising with a swim set. The problem with kickboard drills is that the board interferes with the natural rolling action of your hips.

4. This drill will give you practice kicking on your side. Position yourself on your side in the water. Stretch one arm forward and rest your head on the shoulder of that arm. Stretch your other arm down on the upper part of your body. Keep your arms well stretched to maintain a good body position. Watch that your hips are leaning slightly toward your stomach. Be sure that your kick is aimed outward and downward. Kick about 25 metres on one side, then change to the other side. Repeat this several times.

   Practise this drill in a more realistic swimming position by turning more on your front. To keep your arms in the required position, you will need to kick a little harder. Practising your breathing with this drill will give you a little body roll as well.

Change your body position about every five metres by sliding your arms under your body.

5. For the most advanced kicking drill, assume the front glide position, lock your hands together over the small of your back and keep your chin at water level. Your kicking should be at sprinting speed. This drill requires a lot of energy. Practise it in short sets and have a relaxing swim between sets.

Arm action

In the freestyle, it's mainly your arms that move you through the water. Your arm strokes must be evenly timed to keep your speed up and cut down on the amount of energy you need to do the work. If your stroking is uneven, your speed will vary and so will your body position. This speeding up and slowing down will tire you and affect your performance.

Sculling

Another important concept in the arm movement is *sculling* with your hands. Just as you now use your feet to scull and propel yourself when you kick, your hands can scull during the arm movement and increase your speed. Why does this help your speed? As your hands move through the water, they are most effective if the water resistance is always at a maximum.

Traditionally, swimmers have been taught the concept of "pull and push" which implies that once your hand makes contact with the water, it will move the same block of water back as it progresses through the stroke. Your first attempt to move this block of water will meet a lot of resistance. But as the block progresses the resistance to moving it will be reduced and your body will slow down. If you constantly change the angle of your hand by sculling, your hand will always be moving new blocks of water and the resistance your hand meets will be the same. This steady, high resistance will push you through the water faster.

Sculling with your hands achieves the same effect in the water as a boat propeller does. A propeller is designed to allow water to pass through, so the blades can meet new "still" blocks of water. As the propeller turns, the blades move forward and grab hold of new water. Try to imitate the movement of the blades of the propeller with the sculling motion of your hands. These sculling movements, from side-to-side and up and down with properly angled hands, will propel you forward in the water. More advanced swimmers are taught to think of this as hydrodynamic lift forward.

A uniform stroking speed will keep you moving smoothly and make the best use of your energy. If you want to speed up and win a race, you need to increase the pace of your stroking. To do this, your arm must accelerate as it moves through the water (and not just because your hand has met with less resistance). At every

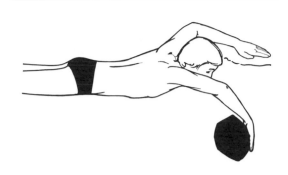

Fig. 1.6. Blocks of water act as resistance on the sculling hand.

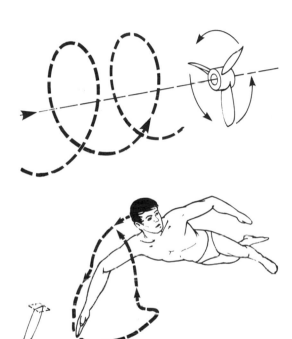

Fig. 1.7. The propeller and the sculling hand.

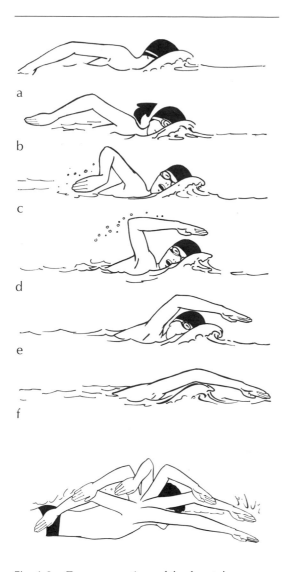

Fig. 1.8. Two perspectives of the freestyle recovery arm sequence. Note high shoulder and elbow positions.

change in the angle of your hand, the speed at which your hand moves should also increase.

Learning tip
Think "sculling" by imitating the movement of the propeller, as you move your hands from side-to-side and up and down.

Practise continuous, low heart rate swimming while you are learning the fine points of the armstroke. (See page 134 to determine your heart rate.) This will help you maintain good control of the relaxed recovery movement. Recover the shoulder first and keep your elbow high, with the recovering arm loose and controlled.

The recovery phase
The roll of your body, as your arms enter and leave the water will make your shoulders appear to be out of the water. A further lift of your shoulder, like an upward shrug, will raise your upper arm, elbow, wrist and hand. The shrug will keep your elbow high and your shoulder will continue to shift forward to bring your elbow to its peak height with the rest of your arm and hand following loosely. Your hand should be level with your shoulder. As your hand swings opposite your shoulder, it will take over the recovery lead and you will begin to stretch your shoulder. Keep your hand and forearm relaxed throughout the recovery phase. In the last few centimetres, your arm will become firm, but not tense, as it shapes itself for the entry — in line with your shoulder, hand turned slightly to enter thumb-first, without a splash. If your arm is tense during recovery, you will find yourself cutting a wide arm path and throwing your body alignment off.

The entry/catch phase
Your hand should enter the water in line with your shoulder. Turn it slightly at the wrist to allow the thumb side to enter first. This cuts down the possibility of carrying air bubbles in your palm — bubbles that will interfere with the effectiveness of your hand as you propel yourself by moving the water. Your hand should be flat and slip into the water without a splash. Your elbow will be slightly raised and your arm will enter the water smoothly. The order of entry is wrist-forearm-elbow.

As your arm begins its forward-downward path, as if reaching over a barrel, you will feel the water's resistance against your palm —as though your hand has "caught" the water. This phase of your arm movement is very important because it sets up the power phase. As you begin the arm stroke, stretch your arm forward, right through your shoulder.

The first power phase

In the power phase, it is the sculling action of your hands that propels you. Following the catch, your hand does a minor scull outward, no more than a few centimetres. (See Figure 1.11, positions a, b) This move is an easy and natural response to the roll of your body. It is important because it is the beginning of the power phase and must not be neglected.

The mid power phase

The next phase begins with an inward scull of your hand. By changing the angle of your hand, you immediately begin the inward scull. Keep your elbow high and pointing away from your body. During this inward scull, your shoulder will still be stretching forward to free your arm to scull. The sculling speed of this phase will gradually increase, reaching its peak when your hand is closest to your chest.

During the in-scull, it is important that your hand not cross the mid-line of your body (the imaginary line between your chin and your navel). If your hand crosses this line, your elbow will drop and the effectiveness of the sculling action will be lost as the water slips off your hand. (See Figure 1.10 and Figure 1.11, position e.)

At the end of the in-scull, your hand, elbow and shoulder should be lined up vertically. At this point, the in-scull continues as an up-scull without interruption. The pitch or angle of your hand will change from inward to up and backward. This change in angle is very important in maintaining firm contact with the water. Your elbow should stay high. (See Figure 1.11, positions d, e.)

The final power phase

At the beginning of the final power phase, your whole arm should begin to move as a unit, so that your hand continues to generate speed. Angle your hand outward and backward in the sculling motion, as your elbow begins to move toward your side. This will pull your hand up and back in preparation for the final scull.

As your elbow reaches your side, your hand will follow into the final inward scull, in preparation for the recovery. (See Figure 1.11, positions g, h.) The rolling action of your body and the bend at your elbow will make this move feel natural. Keep your hand moving until it reaches the bottom edge of your swimsuit, with the palm of your hand facing your thigh. During the last few

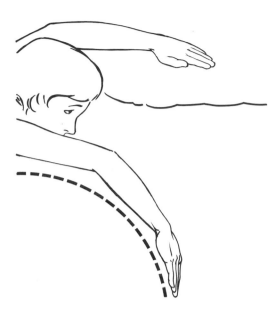

Fig. 1.9. The over-the-barrel freestyle entry and catch.

Fig. 1.10. Front view of freestyle mid point of power phase. Note arm does not cross mid-line.

Fig. 1.11. Freestyle underwater arm action sequence.

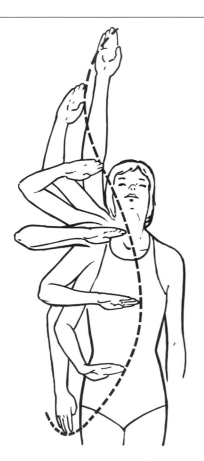

Fig. 1.12. The "S" pattern of freestyle underwater hand path.

centimetres of this move, your elbow should extend further to ensure a smooth finish and transition into the recovery.

> *Learning tip*
> While your arm is under water, think of drawing a large "S". This will help you change the angle of your hand and change the block of water your palm is moving. Keep your hand naturally open. Do not cup it.

> *Learning tip*
> While doing your stroke, remember that one of your hands is always holding onto the water (sculling), while the other may be recovering or just entering. This way you will always provide continuity in your propulsion.

Timing of the arms

Stroke timing determines when one arm is entering in relation to the other arm. To move smoothly and continuously, you must always keep your strokes accurately timed. The water resistance on one hand should be well engaged while the other hand is preparing to let go of the resistance.

Because each arm must prepare for the power phase through the entry and catch, the arms will overlap slightly. This overlap means that both arms are in the water at the same time. One arm is entering and the other arm is either midway in the power phase or just finishing it. (See Figure 1.13 a, b.) How much you overlap your strokes will depend on your experience and the type of swimming you are doing. For distance swimming, most swimmers favour more overlap, so that the entering and stroking hands are closer together. For sprinting, the two hands should be further apart, but still overlapping. The slight timing differences between distance and sprint swimming are related to the speed of the arm movements. In distance swimming the arms move more slowly, so more overlap is possible.

Drills

1. Get used to your arm movements before you go into the water. Stand straight and stretch one arm over your head and the other along your side. Practise your stroke by bringing your arm straight down to shoulder level, palm down, fingers pointing forward. Turn your hand inward and bring it nearly against your chest, keeping your elbow at shoulder height. Turn your hand down and begin to extend your arm. As your elbow is brought toward your side, your hand will continue to move to the side to the level of your swimsuit.

Fig. 1.13. Freestyle arm action timing: (a) closer overlap timing; (b) farther apart overlap timing.

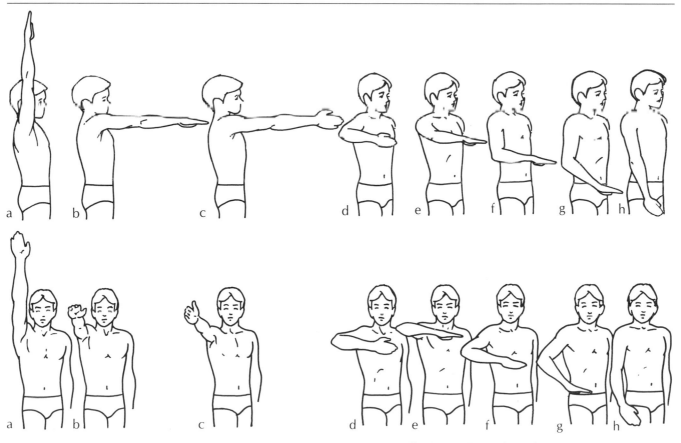

Fig. 1.14. Freestyle stroke pattern accuracy drill.

a

b

c

d

e

f

g

h

Fig. 1.15. One-arm freestyle arm action sequence.

Practise this with each arm. Have your instructor or a friend check to make sure your elbow stays high during the first three parts of the stroke.

Practise this drill with your eyes closed and concentrate until you can feel the stroke positions.

2. Practise one-arm freestyle to focus on one aspect of the stroke at a time. Extend your resting arm in front of your body and keep your eyes on the base of your thumb. This will keep your head in position and set a target for your arm's entry. Remember to stretch your arm forward through your shoulder during entry. Work on recovery and entry for one length. During the next length, focus on the catch and the power phase; another length on the power phase and the finish; and so on. This drill limits the ability of your body to roll, so don't devote too much time to it.

A variation on this drill is with the resting arm extended back along the side of your body. This drill will make you conscious of your legs, which will have to work harder. You will also have to concentrate more on the position of your head and the entry process because your hand will not be up front to guide you. This is an advanced drill, not to be practised until you have mastered the first version.

3. As a variation on the one-arm drill, after a long entry by the stroking arm, switch it with the resting arm and continue the resting arm through the stroke. The long entry is accomplished by attempting to reach beyond the resting arm, as if your moving arm was made out of rubber. This drill will help you learn long, relaxed stroking and continuous kicking.

4. This drill, called "chicken wings", works best after you have developed reasonable kicking ability. Even if you haven't, you should be able to do it for short distances. Make your hands into fists and tuck them under your arms to make wings. Swim with your elbows instead of your hands. The rolling action of your body and continuous kicking will help you. The drill will emphasize the use of your shoulders to initiate the recovery phase and help you to stretch your shoulders.

5. Try an arms-only drill to concentrate on the arm action and learn the feel of the different forces acting on your arm. Place a flotation device between your legs to keep them from helping. Swim only a few lengths like this and always follow up with kicking and full stroke swimming. This way no one aspect of the stroke will become more important than another.

For a variation on this drill, try it with your hands fisted to make your forearms, as well as your hands, propel you.

Points to remember about the freestyle arm action

- During the recovery phase, keep your arms loose and close to your body, with your elbows bent and higher than your hands.
- At the entry, keep your elbows higher than your hands as if you were reaching over a barrel.
- During the underwater phase, remember to bend your elbows and gradually speed up your sculling hands to develop a powerful stroke.
- At the end of your stroke, be prepared to breathe with a roll of your body.

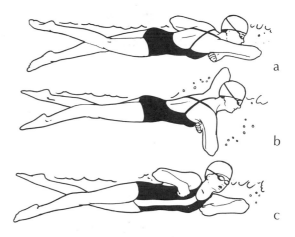

Fig. 1.16. Freestyle chicken wings drill. Note good shoulder lift, strong kicking.

Breathing

When you breathe during the freestyle, it should be a comfortable inhale-exhale rhythm, not an exaggerated deep breath taken as often as possible because your face is momentarily submerged. How deep a breath you take and how often you do it will depend on how hard you swim. There are many options for freestyle breathing. As you practise to build up your other skills, you will learn which breathing patterns you prefer.

Your head should move to follow the roll of your body with a small additional roll to the side when you take a breath. This will help you to keep your body in line and your head in a comfortable position. Practise breathing on both sides to keep your body roll balanced and rhythmical.

Do not lift your head to take a breath. Instead, your head should rotate with the rest of your body. *Inhale* at the end of the power phase, when your shoulder is at its highest point in the move from the power phase to recovery. Your head and body will roll to the side, as your arm begins the recovery phase. (See Figure 1.8, positions b, c, d.)

Take a deep, quick breath through your mouth that forces the air into your lungs. Don't keep the air inside your cheeks like a food-hoarding hamster. You need the air in your lungs and it is important to get it there immediately. As your arm passes your head, and your hand takes the lead, the breath should be completed and your face will rotate back into the water. The timing of your breathing is very important. To swim effectively, it must not interfere with the rolling motion of your body.

Exhale as your body begins to rotate to the opposite side. Blow the air out steadily through both your mouth and your nose, until it's time to take the next breath. Blow the last wisp of air out forcefully so you don't inhale any water trapped on your lips.

The breathing pattern you use depends on whether you are swimming competitively, the distance that is covered and the

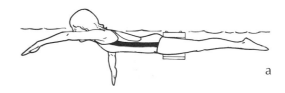

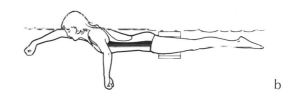

Fig. 1.17. Arms only (a) and fisted (b) freestyle arm action drill.

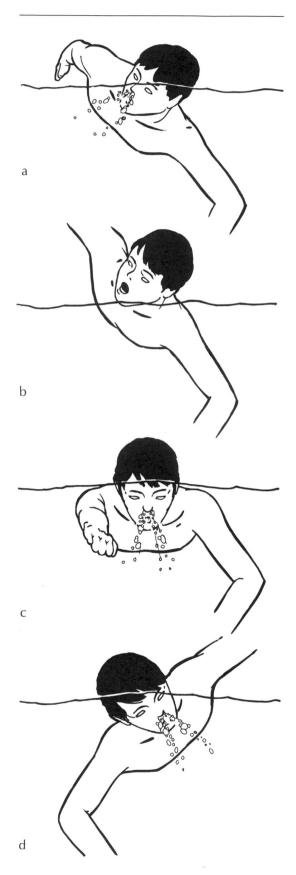

a

b

c

d

Fig. 1.18. Freestyle breathing action. Note rolling shoulders and head.

pattern you are comfortable with. In the *normal breathing pattern*, a breath is taken on every right arm or every left arm. The problem with this pattern is that you may develop a lopsided stroke—the "breathing" arm will have a high elbow during recovery and the "non-breathing" arm will be very flat. When this happens, the roll of your body is minimal and your stroke suffers.

In the *alternate breathing pattern*, you breathe on every third arm, alternating left and right. This pattern preserves your natural rolling rhythm and allows you to see the swimmers on either side of you. This breathing pattern is good for longer distance training or competition. As you become more experienced, the pattern can be changed for longer breath control, waiting for every fifth, seventh or ninth arm. Instructors encourage advanced swimmers to adopt this pattern because it develops the ability to withstand the pain of not breathing and helps block the desire to take a breath. During competition, in the turns or the final 10 metres, you need a high degree of breath control.

For short races, limited but planned breathing is best. The frequency with which you draw breath depends on what you have practised and what you are comfortable with. Swimmers should breathe only on one side in short races, on every second, third, fourth or even fifth right or left arm. This limited breathing while sprinting, when the stroke frequency is high, will keep your body aligned and drag will be at a minimum.

For longer races, 200 metres or more, your goal is to keep yourself from creating an early oxygen debt.

(An oxygen debt is created when you neglect to breathe often enough while swimming hard to allow your body to filter out the waste products it builds up as it works. It's like having dirty gasoline in the tank of a car: the car starts to sputter and slow down. Similarly, your body will slow down and eventually stop if deprived of oxygen.)

Most swimmers prefer some form of alternate breathing pattern to keep their stroke rhythm even and allow them to see the competition. Before the freestyle race, choose the best breathing pattern for the stroke and distance, and stick with it.

Learning tip
Breathing must not be taken for granted. It should be practised as much as your arm stroke and kicking skills. Learn all the variations, so you can adapt to the various distances and speeds. Practise each breathing variation during your training sessions.

Drills

1. Before you try any one breathing pattern, you must be able to release inhaled air under water. This may sound elementary, but many swimmers cannot keep up controlled breathing pat-

terns for long because they have not practised the fundamentals of breath control. Practise inhaling and then blowing all the air out under water.

The next step is to establish a rhythmical inhale-exhale pattern by bobbing up and down. Practise this drill for about 15 seconds and gradually increase the time until it equals the time it takes you to swim two lengths of the pool.

2. Swimmers often lift their heads to breathe, instead of rotating to the side. Practise on the deck by lying on stacked kickboards and have someone check your head movements. This practice will not include the body roll, but you should get a feel for the rotation and the breathing rhythm. Try it with one arm stretched forward and one arm back. Rotate your head to the side with the back stretched arm and then change the arm position. Repeat the drill again in waist-deep water by leaning forward. This will make the drill more realistic as you inhale and exhale with your face in the water.

3. Swimmers always have a preferred breathing side, but you must be able to breathe easily on both sides. The drill used to develop this skill is simple. While swimming lengths, always breathe facing the same wall of the pool. This will ensure that you breathe to the left for one length, and to the right for the next one.

Points to remember about freestyle breathing

- Never lift your head to take a breath.
- Rotate your head to the side when taking a breath to keep the head aligned with the rest of your body.
- Take a normal breath and allow the air to enter your lungs.
- Start blowing the air out slowly into the water as soon as you have completed your inhalation.

Learning progression
When you are learning the freestyle stroke—or any other stroke—start with the simple skills that are the basis of the more complex movements. Here is a list of the skills that have been described so far in the order they should be learned, following a developmental progression—from the easy and basic to the difficult and complex. At each stage, always do short swims first for easy control.

1. Good *body position* is the key to efficient swimming with a minimum of drag, helping to conserve energy and enabling you to swim faster. First try the body position on the pool deck, lying on a few kickboards to get a feel for it. Then try it in the water, with a strong push from the wall, making sure that your

shoulders and hips are near the surface of the water, your head is high and your eyes looking forward.

2. Now you can add *kicking* to the body position. Kicking should be done first without the board and while holding your breath. Once you have mastered the basics and wish to build endurance, practise with the board.

3. Once body position and proper kicking have been established, add the *arm stroke*. Read the description carefully and make sure you have the general idea before you enter the water. Try the one arm action while standing on the deck first and then while standing in the water. When you understand the mechanics of the arm stroke, practise the one-arm stroke with kicking. Try the different one-arm drills, but always make sure that your kicking is continuous and your body position is correct.

4. When you can perform the above skills with ease and confidence, concentrate on your *breathing* pattern to find the one that is most appropriate and interferes least with your stroke.

5. *Continuous arm action* is the next skill level and combines all the previous ones. Remember to look forward in order to see the entering hand. Kick continuously. Move your hand through the water progressively faster. Roll your body. Breathe at the end of the stroke and relax your arm during recovery.

The freestyle start

In freestyle, and all the other strokes, a good fast start will lead into a fast swim. For swimmers in individual races, the most popular start is the *grab start*. However, for relay racing the *wind-up* start, which has a full arm swing, is used by the second, third and fourth swimmers in a team.

The objective of the start is to move off the starting block as quickly as possible, get yourself into the proper body position immediately after entering the water and begin to generate speed.

The grab start technique

Your initial position on the block is defined by the rules of competition. If the "no false start" rule is being used for the race you may be positioned on the front edge of the starting block, so all swimmers can take the "mark" at the same time. Anybody who breaks away before the sound of the gun is disqualified.

But the more common rule of starting the race is to stand at the back of the starting block, and move to the front edge when the command "take your mark" is given. In this case, because the swimmers are moving forward at different speeds to take the "mark", false starts are common. Therefore, two false starts are allowed before a swimmer is disqualified.

The difference between the rules is only at the initial position.

You are either at the front edge or at the back of the block. If you are at the front edge, on the command "take your mark", bend forward and grasp the block. If you are at the back of the block, on the command "take your mark", step forward, bend down and grasp the block — all in the same motion. When you are at the front of the block, your toes should curl down over the edge and your feet be placed about the width of your hips apart. Your grasp on the starting block will either be between your feet or just outside your feet. In this "down" position, you will be bent forward, legs slightly bent but not squatting. Your chest will be close to your thighs and your head will be almost at knee level, but looking in front of your knees. Your hips will be slightly higher than your head.

At the sound of the gun, take off from the block with a powerful drive. To do this, grasp the block very firmly and pull. Your head will drop between your knees and your hips will rise even higher. Your body will tip forward, ready to fly off the block. As your body tips, release the edge, bend your knees a little more for the drive off the block. Swing your arms in front and stretch your body forward and up. Your "lift off" from the block will be in a slightly upward direction, as if you were trying to fly over a fence. (See Figure 1.19, positions b, c.)

> *Learning tip*
> Learn to *jump away* from the starting block to increase your distance at the start.

Fig. 1.19. Grab start technique.

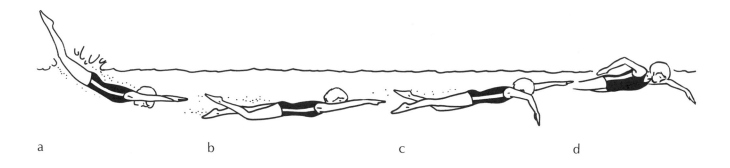

a   b   c   d

Fig. 1.20. Freestyle start: (a) entry; (b) glide kick; (c) kick-first stroke; (d) second stroke on surface.

Your arms will keep moving forward until your body reaches the peak of its flight. Once at the peak, your arms will stop and point at the spot in the water where you will enter. Bend at your hips to allow your upper body to line up with your arms. As you enter the water, bend your legs at the knees a little to flip them slightly upwards. Your body will level out under water in response to this leg move. Use a dolphin-like movement to move your legs back to align with your body. The sequential bending and straightening of your knees is important, because it helps you to assume a streamlined body position and get ready for the first stroke quickly.

During entry, make sure that your whole body slips through the same small hole in the water without any splash. Pretend you are going through a ring buoy. Your dive should be about one metre deep or less, and you should not be under the water for long. It is a good idea to be at the surface after about four to five kicks.

Learning tip
Keep your body streamlined in the air and during the entry into the water. Work to improve the distance and speed of your glide from the starting block. Have someone time you to see if your dive is improving.

After entry, line up into a long, streamlined body position and glide until you begin to lose speed. Start kicking before you begin stroking to maintain the speed of your dive. Then begin your arm strokes. As the first arm stroke begins, your head will still be under water. This first stroke, accompanied by a slight elevation of your head, will pull your body to the surface. (See Figure 1.20.) Never take a breath on the first arm stroke. It is best if you do not breathe for the first two or three arm movements.

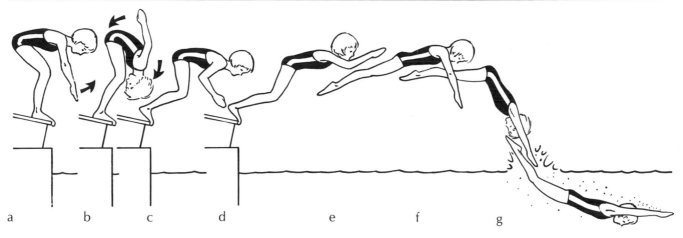

Fig. 1.21. Full-arm swing start: (a) take your mark;
(b) the gun; (c,d) take-off; (e,f) flight; (g) entry.

The full-arm swing start technique

This starting technique is very similar to the grab start. But in this start, the movement of your head and arms is what tips your body off balance and into flight.

The initial position on the block is the same as in the grab start. At the command "take your mark", step to the front edge of the block and bend forward, taking your upper body to near horizontal level. Your arms hang loosely in front of your chest and your knees are bent slightly, hips high. At the sound of the gun, bend forward until your forehead nearly touches your knees, and swing your arms forward and outward in a circle. As your arms pass your knees, lift your head and move it forward, as your knees are extending.

Learning tip
Always pick the spot where your body will enter the water and keep looking at it.

Points to remember about the freestyle start

- Bend your knees for a very strong push-off from the starting block.
- Kick almost as soon as you hit the water.
- Start your first arm stroke while your body is still under water but rising, so you will not be too deep.
- Hold your breath on the first two or three arm strokes and kick very hard.

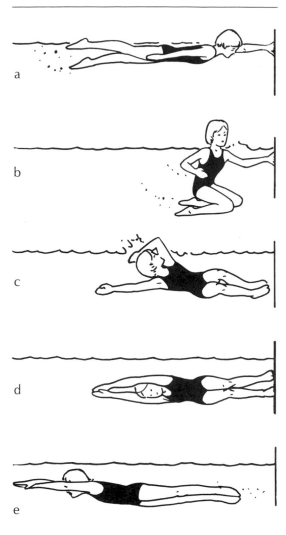

a

b

c

d

e

Fig. 1.22. Freestyle open turn technique.

Drills
Most swimmers are able to dive into the water head first, so there is seldom any need for elementary drills. These drills are designed to emphasize the clean entry concept or "going through the hole" with the entire body.

1. Practise diving through a plastic hula hoop from a height, perhaps from a diving board. Once you can do this smoothly, try the same dive from the starting block.

2. Practise the grab start from the one-metre diving board. The spring of the board will help you to attain good height so you can practise the pike position at the peak of your flight. For a good pike position, your body should be bent at the waist, as in Figure 1.19, position f. If you're feeling adventurous, try this with the plastic hoop to get a clean entry.

3. To make sure you stretch out during entry, practise the two starts from the starting block over a stretched-out rope or the reaching pole commonly found in swimming pools.
Never practise your dives in shallow water.

The freestyle turn
The turn in the freestyle stroke, as in all other strokes, is a fast reversal of direction and uses the end wall to generate speed. You can generate more speed at the turn than during the actual swim, so it is extremely important to do the turn properly. A well-exe-cuted turn should take about one second to perform. Once you have become confident in your ability to do a smooth turn, you should be able to kick hard during both the approach and departure from the wall.

The two most commonly used turns in freestyle are the *open turn* or learning turn and the *roll-flip turn*. Only the latter is used for competition.

The objectives of any turn are to maintain the continuity and rhythm of your stroke and to increase your speed as your body moves off the wall.

> *Learning tip*
> Always approach the turn without giving up speed.

The open turn technique
Reach your touching arm forward to the wall to take hold of the lip of the pool or simply place your palm on the wall. Your touch-ing hand will reach slightly away from the line of its shoulder, past the head, almost in line with the opposite shoulder. Mean-while the opposite hand (still in the water) will sweep minimally

across your back. These movements work together to rotate the front part of your body away from the wall. The hand on the wall then quickly pushes away from the wall hard to join your other hand, while your hips swing toward the wall like a pendulum. At the same time, your legs are drawn up under your seat. When your arms are side-by-side, they simply reach into the glide position to be ready for the push-off.

Place your feet on the wall sideways and push off immediately. When you push off, you will be on your side and should roll onto your stomach into a long, streamlined glide. Start kicking as soon as you know you're clear of the wall. It is important to practise the touch to the wall with each arm.

> *Learning tip*
> Never take a breath on the last arm stroke before the turn or on the first arm stroke after the turn.

The roll-flip turn technique

The approach of this turn is similar to the open turn. However, instead of reaching for the wall, the recovering hand of the last arm stroke will continue into the entry. Your head dives along with your entering arm. At this time, the opposite arm stops at its respective hip. (See Figure 1.23, position a.) When your head is pointing downward, reverse both your hands and pull them toward your head.

> *Learning tip*
> Tuck your body to allow quick rotation, but do not get into a tight ball.

At this point, your legs are no longer kicking. The diving action of your head and the reversed pull of your hands will start a somersault action, similar to a forward roll on the floor. At this point in the turn you should be able to see your knees. (See Figure 1.23, position b.)

> *Learning tip*
> Keep your arms close to your chest during the roll-flip part of the turn.

Tuck your knees to your chest for a tight forward roll toward the wall. Your buttocks will roll slightly over the surface of the water. When you have almost rolled onto your back, begin to reach your legs toward the wall for the push-off. As your legs reach toward

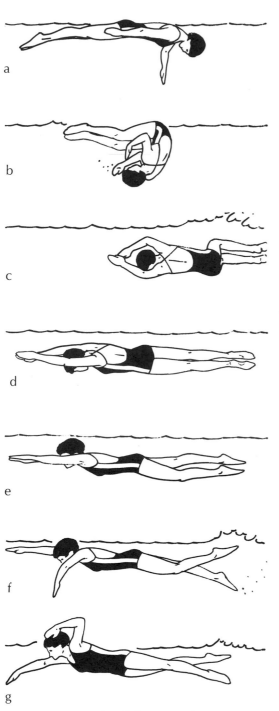

Fig. 1.23. Freestyle roll-flip turn technique.

the wall, they should be prepared to push off as soon as the balls of your feet are in firm contact with the wall. Place your feet sideways, one on top of the other, on the wall, in preparation for the push. With your feet sideways, your body is lined up on its side, ready for the push-off — a powerful stretch of your legs to speed you through the water. The rest of the action is similar to the open turn.

Learning tip
Always leave the wall long and streamlined.

Points to remember about the freestyle turn

- Kick hard in and out of the turn.
- The turn should add to your speed and not slow you down.
- During training, always use the proper turn technique, just as you would in competition.

Drills

1. Practise the forward roll on a mat, until you can stand up with your legs together and without the help of your hands.

2. Practise the forward roll in the water by jumping off the pool bottom. Land on your back and stretch your legs toward an imaginary wall.

3. Glide toward the pool end wall and do a forward roll about one arm's length away. Remember to paddle backwards with your hands to help the roll-flip action. Land on your back and push out on your back, legs kicking hard, with your arms stretched over your head and covering your ears. This will help you to streamline your body.

4. Continue drill number 3, but this time twist your body to position your feet sideways on the wall. Push out on your side with strong kicking and roll onto your stomach with your arms stretched forward, while you look at the base of your thumbs.

2. THE BREASTSTROKE

Alex talks about the breaststroke

The breaststroke has always been my favourite stroke and is probably the one I swim best. I feel that a good breaststroke is crucial in individual medley competition, mainly because it's possible to make up a lot of time during this stroke.

My first competitive race as a youngster was the 50-metre breaststroke. Unfortunately, I was disqualified for not touching the wall with two hands. I cried for about 15 minutes after that race, but luckily, the experience did not deter me from continuing to swim the breaststroke.

Timing is very important for good technique in the breaststroke. One drill that helped my timing was a catch-up breaststroke. During this exercise, I would perform the pull and kick of the stroke separately, one after the other. This gave me a better feel for the sculling action of my arms and the thrusting action of my legs.

FACTS ABOUT THE BREASTSTROKE

The breaststroke is the slowest competitive stroke, but it requires the most energy. In competitive swimming, the breaststroke has more rules than any other stroke and these restrictions reduce its instinctive, flowing movement.

The many rules are designed to standardize the stroke and eliminate innovations that may give the swimmer an unfair advantage. The restrictions still allow a great deal of freedom for the swimmer to decide on a style that best suits his or her body type and the distance to be swum.

The two styles of breaststroke most commonly used are the *natural breaststroke* (sometimes called the undulating breaststroke) and the *orthodox breaststroke* (sometimes called the flat breaststroke). In the natural breaststroke, the shoulder is kept high in the forward stretched position, with an undulating body and a very low head position. This allows for a much more natural flow of the body.

In the orthodox breaststroke the body is kept very flat. More than the natural breaststroke, it takes advantage of the body's buoyancy and consequently conserves energy. The natural breaststroke is more suitable for the 200-metre distance, although swimmers have been successful with this style at the 100-metre distance as well. It is the orthodox breaststroke that should be used in competition for the breaststroke portion of the individual medley.

When you learn the breaststroke, concentrate on the general concept of the different movements. Put your whole body into the stroke and remember the natural floating ability of your body. The fine points and competitive restrictions can be studied and practised after you have mastered the basics.

The background

One of the earliest forms of swimming was a type of breaststroke. There is evidence that it was used about 1000 to 500 BC. Though it has changed over the years, with different combinations of arm and leg techniques, the breaststroke was always done on the chest, with most of the action placed on the legs. More recently, the arm action became more important, with the shoulders kept low and flat. This new, faster form of the breaststroke was developed by Dr. James Counsilman at the University of Indiana.

The modern breaststroke was performed for the first time at the 1908 Summer Olympic Games.

The action

Good breaststroke technique uses your arms and legs to create continuous motion and takes advantage of your body's natural floating ability. Your arms and legs move at different times in this stroke, each within its own cycle. While your arms are stroking, your legs recover. And while your legs are driving, your arms recover. Both arms and legs contribute to your speed. Your head must break the surface of the water during every stroke cycle, except at the start and during turns when special rules allow you to stay under water.

The hands and arms, from a stretched forward position, make an upside-down and diagonally sloping heart shape in their stroke. The legs and feet are lifted behind the buttocks and extended backward in a circle. The feet act like a propeller, moving from a completely stretched out position to a completely stretched inward position. The resulting kick should give you a feeling of a thrusting stretch forward through your trunk and arms.

Objectives for the breaststroke

- Maintain constant speed in both the arm and leg actions.
- Take advantage of the natural floating ability of the body without changing the mechanics of the stroke action.
- Your arms should provide the speed for this stroke.
- Your legs should control and support your body and continue the speed begun by your arms.

THE TECHNIQUE

Body position

Your body's motion in the breaststroke is different from its motion in the freestyle. Instead of rolling from side to side, your body will *undulate* (ripple) from head to toe, as though you were trying to ride the waves. This is a controlled up and down movement of your head and shoulders that works with your kicking and arm strokes to make you roll like a wave through the water.

The breaststroke—probably my favourite stroke.

MARCO CHIESA

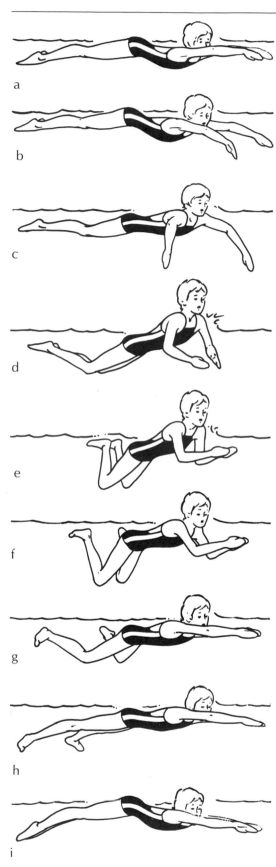

Fig. 2.1. Body position sequence in the breast-stroke.

To carry out this undulation smoothly, drop your head to the surface or slightly below the surface of the water at the forward extension of the arms. At the same time, the legs and feet will be finishing their inward sweeping and flipping action. The drop of the shoulders and action of the feet will bring the hips to the surface of the water. When you take a breath at the end of the arm stroke, your head and shoulders will also come up high. This up and down movement of your head and shoulders and your hips combined with the forward movement of your body will make your body appear to undulate.

Although your body rises and falls as you move through the water, it is important to stay close to the surface, so that you can feel a little water wash over your head. Keep your shoulders level, so you can slide through the water without much drag.

The trunk position

From the hips forward, your body works as a unit. Your stomach area and chest serve as the floating surface, like the bottom of a boat. Keep your hips close to the water's surface and keep them even as you glide forward.

In the breaststroke, the arms are considered part of the trunk and have no basic position. They are like paddles and operate independently of the boat (the body). The arms, when stretched forward, are placed at the same level as the shoulders.

> *Learning tip*
> Keep your whole body close to the surface, even after you learn to undulate.

The head position

Your head moves with your shoulders in one unit. The rules let you keep your head under the water. So line your head up with your arms when you do your long, drag-reducing stretch forward.

> *Learning tip*
> Always look ahead and over your arms as they stretch forward. Your head should be just below the surface.

The leg position

In the breaststroke, your legs work together on the same level. There is no one proper leg position within this stroke. There is a series of positions that will be discussed later in detail. As you perform the leg action, remember that your legs should not create more drag by unnecessarily increasing the space your body takes up in the water. Keep your legs as close to both the line of your body and the surface as good technique allows.

Learning tip
Keep your leg movements long to keep yourself in a good horizontal body position.

Points to remember about the breaststroke body position

- Stay long and loose.
- Keep your head lined up with your shoulders, except when you breathe in.
- Allow your feet to float toward the surface after the kick.

Drills
Similar drills to those in the "Body position" section of the freestyle stroke may be used to establish a streamlined body in the water. Practise gliding with the head up and down to note the different effect on the body. This will help you with the undulation and the positioning of your head.

Leg action
The kick in the breaststroke contributes more power than the kick in any other stroke, so it must be learned precisely. Both your legs work at the same time, on the same level. They take over from your arms as they finish their stroke, in a continuous cycle of movement. If you keep up this rhythm, there will be no pause in your forward progress. Your legs control and support your body position. They also maintain the speed generated by your arms.

Learning tip
Do flexibility exercises every day to keep your hips, ankles and feet loose and moving easily.

The recovery phase
Since the basic body position is the glide position, the legs must recover before they can drive. In the recovery phase, keep your knees about the width of your hips apart and lift your heels toward your buttocks, toes touching and heels separated, allowing your knees to drop enough to keep your feet under water. When your feet are nearly touching your buttocks, turn your toes outward and down. Spread your feet apart, wider than your knees and ready for the next thigh stretch, and kick. Keep your feet under the water during the recovery. (See Figure 2.2, positions b, c, d.)

Learning tip
Keep a mental image of the proper mechanics of your kick and practise it in your mind.

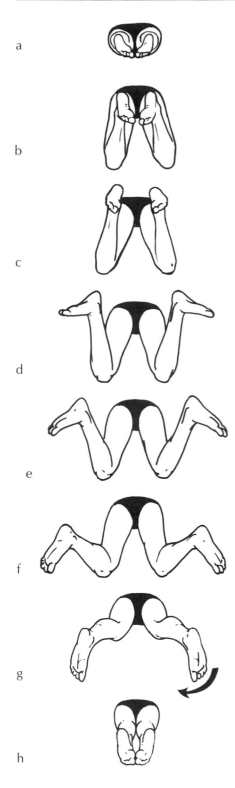

a

b

c

d

e

f

g

h

Fig. 2.2.   Rear view of kick sequence.

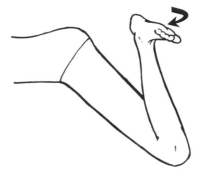

Fig. 2.3.   Side view of Fig. 2.2., position d.

The drive phase

At the beginning of the kick, your knees will be bent and spread the width of your hips apart. Your heels should be close to your buttocks, toes touching and heels separated. Move your knees up and slightly backward to stretch your thighs back and start the kick. Feel the water with your inner thighs before you begin to move your feet.

Turn your feet outward and down. Making sure that your legs move together, sweep your legs back, keeping your knees at the same width and allowing your feet to move outward. Keep your feet turned out and down during this sweep to push against the water with your instep.

Rotate your feet inward as your legs straighten out. Your feet will move in a circular path like propellers, through fresh, resistant blocks of water. When your feet come together, snap them in and upward to provide the final thrust and bring your thighs back up to a horizontal position. Your feet should accelerate continually as they go through the kick. At the end of the kick, your legs and toes will be stretched into a long glide position.

> ### Learning tip
> In competitive breaststroke, the term "glide" refers to a stretched position rather than an actual glide. Gliding would break the continuity of movement and speed, and is not used in a race.

Drills

While you are learning the kick with these drills, hold your breath for a few sequences so you can concentrate on the action a little better. When you are more familiar with the kicking action, include the breathing action as well. With these drills, always breathe when the feet have completed their final inward flip and are stretched out. To take a breath, stretch and raise your chin forward to clear the water, take a breath and return your face to the water for the next kick.

1. On a table or a safely elevated board, lie on your stomach and have someone guide you through the correct technique, especially the circular path of your feet. Practise until you can perform it easily on land.

2. Move into the pool and hold onto the edge as someone guides you through the correct mechanics of the kick. Keep your face in the water, take a deep breath and hold it so you can look back under your chest to see how the move looks. Repeat as many kicks as you can in one breath.

3. Glide on your back with your arms stretched over your head and your hands clasped. Do breaststroke kicking on your back and remember to stay in a perfectly horizontal position.

    This drill concentrates on the heel lift during recovery. Because you are on your back, your heels will drop, in an upside-down version of the heel lift. Use this drill to help you learn to perform the kick symmetrically, that is, both legs working together. In order to be technically correct, your knees *must* remain under water, with your stomach kept close to the surface.

4. Take a deep breath, hold it and push off from the bottom of the pool in the front glide position. Kick four or five times and stop. Do short distances and check the mechanics of your kick. For this drill, keep your arms perfectly straight to duplicate the actual arm recovery position. As a variation, clasp your hands together or use a kickboard. Hold your breath for a few kicks. Stop and repeat with another breath.

5. At the more advanced level, swimmers can practise kicking with the *heel touch* technique. This drill will ensure that you lift your ankles high. The arms should be extended at the sides and over the buttocks. Lift your feet up to touch your heels to the tips of your fingers and then kick.

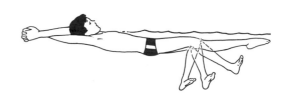

Fig. 2.4.   Upside-down breaststroke kick.

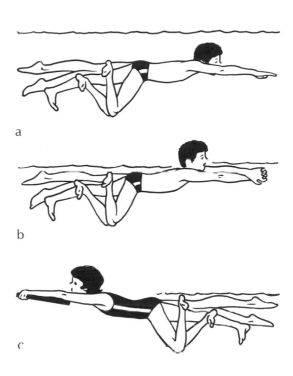

a

b

c

Fig. 2.5.   Breaststroke kick: (a) without board; (b) with clasped hands and wrists crossed — take breath when heels are lifted; (c) with board — take breath when heels are lifted.

Points to remember about the breaststroke leg action

- Always move the legs together and on the same level.
- Push against the water with the instep of your feet.
- Use your feet as propeller blades to keep the water "fresh" for continuous propelling resistance.
- The movement of the feet accelerates continually as they go through the kicking action.

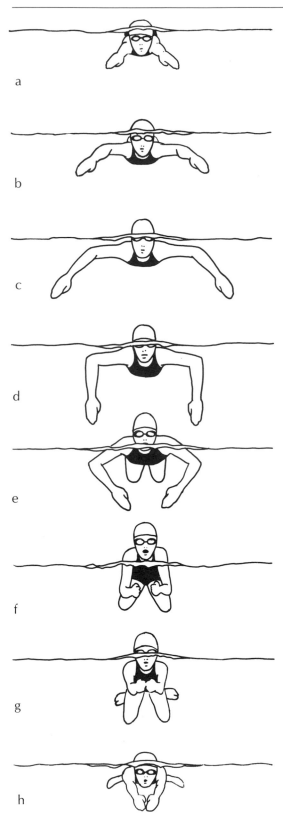

Fig. 2.6.   Breaststroke arm action scull-out and scull-in sequences. The arms in the start and finish positions are stretched forward.

Arm action

Make sure you have mastered the kick before you add the arm action. Just like the action of your legs, your arms stroke together on the same level. As in the freestyle, you scull to make sure your hands move new blocks of water. Again, your arms provide most of the speed. This time they do their work while your legs are recovering from the drive phase.

The timing of the arms and legs is not difficult, but requires some concentration. When your hands and arms are finished with the stroke and are under your chest, begin your heel lift. The arms continue their forward movement as the heels arrive at the buttocks. The final stretch of the arms is co-ordinated with the backward thrust of the feet.

Sculling

During the final thrust of your feet, quickly move your arms forward from under your shoulders and chest into a long stretch, while your feet finish their sweep and snap. During this forward movement, most swimmers keep their palms and fingertips together to form an arrowhead. This movement is a fast shooting action. Your arms should slope down slightly. At the end of the arm stretch turn your hands outward, thumbs down and close together, small fingers up and diagonally pointing to the side, and start an outward scull at your shoulders to keep your arms straight. As you begin the outward sweep, your wrists should be slightly flexed to give you a pulling lift forward, like an aircraft wing. (See Figure 2.7 for arm recovery sequence.)

In order to catch undisturbed water, your arms will not only move out, but also slightly down. As your arms pass the width of your shoulders, your elbows will rise slightly and begin to bend to keep your upper arms and elbows close to the surface. Gradually speed up the outward sculling movement as your arms approach this extreme side point of your arm stroke. Stop your arms' outward movement past your shoulders when you can no longer see your hands.

At the extreme scull-out position, your hands must reverse direction and scull in. Sweep your hands in quickly, leading with your thumbs, followed by your elbows. Keep your elbows high until your hands are at the width of your shoulders, then drop your elbows to follow the path of your hands.

Learning tip
Always think "scull", never "pull".

Learning tip
Your elbows should be higher than your hands, especially during the scull-in phase.

The recovery phase

As your arms enter the shoulder-width area, they will begin their recovery. Bring your hands close together under the upper part of your chest with your thumbs nearly touching. Move your arms forward, elbows close under your body, to create the least amount of resistance. Make this forward move fast, inside the width of your shoulders and slightly downward, finishing with a long stretch while your feet snap in and up, and your hips rise to the surface to begin the next kick phase. Stretch your arms forward and slightly downward from your shoulder joints as you are finishing your kick.

If your arms pause at all, it will be here, when they're fully stretched out at the end of the arm recovery, waiting for your feet to finish their snap. A good, competitive breaststroke will keep the flow of speed — generated first by your arms and then your legs—uninterrupted without any pause. Slowly begin the outward sculling movement and do not wait for the legs to finish completely. If you are a beginner, learn to finish long with a good stretch and don't worry about starting the next phase too quickly.

Learning tip
Imagine that the movement of your arms describes a pattern like a big heart.

a

b

c

Fig. 2.7.   Breaststroke arm recovery sequence.

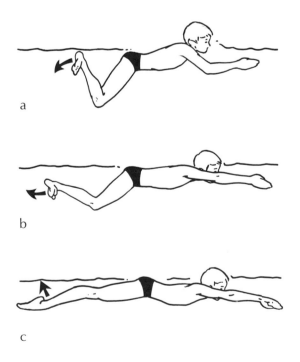

a

b

c

Fig. 2.8.   Breaststroke arm recovery and start of scull-out phase with the finish of kick.

Learning tip
During recovery, your arms and hands should jab forward, as if you were trying to poke a hole in a balloon floating just below the surface.

Points to remember about the breaststroke arm action

- The two arms always work at the same time and on the same level.
- The arms move through a continually accelerating pattern.
- The recovering arms and hands should jab forward forcefully.
- The movement of the arms is continuous. It may stop only at the point of full extension, at the end of the recovery, to wait for the feet to finish their snap.

Drills
1.   For your first drill, stand on the pool deck, bend forward and

have someone guide you through the arm action outlined above. This will help you become familiar with the arm action.

2. For the next drill, stand in the water, waist deep, and practise your arm movements. Bend forward from your waist, so you will be in a realistic body position and can mimic the actual up and down movement of your shoulders.

3. To learn to move your arms around your shoulder joints instead of just at your elbows, try the "arm rotator drill". Hold a buoy between your knees to keep your legs from interfering. Move your arms out and in, sculling without bending your elbows. This will also show you how your hands scull back in on the same level that they sculled out. As you progress, you can bend your elbows during the scull-in phase, a little at first, then progressively more.

4. In this advanced drill, do a dolphin kick for every arm action. This will help you to learn the free flowing action of the body in the breaststroke and get a feel for the required stretch of your upper body as you come out of your kick.

Breathing

While there are different styles of breathing for the freestyle, there is only one option for breathing during the breaststroke. Take a breath when your shoulders are at their highest point, just as your arms have completed their in-sweep. Start breathing out when your arms are stretched forward and your shoulders are back in the water and continue through the stroke. Always blow the air out into the water through both your mouth and your nose.

The actual breathing action is easy, since it is co-ordinated with the upward movement of the shoulders. To provide some assistance to this action, move your chin forward as the shoulders begin to rise. Never lift your head. (See Figure 2.6 position f.)

a

b

c

Fig. 2.9. Arm rotator drill.

Learning tip
Never lift your head to take a breath. Always move your head with your shoulders, as one unit.

Points to remember about breaststroke breathing

- Allow your head to rise with your shoulders.
- Before you begin to inhale, make sure that the last wisp of air is blown out forcefully to avoid swallowing water.
- It is best to breathe on every stroke to make sure that the shoulders keep rising.

Drills

1. For your first drill, squat in the water with your face under the surface. Begin to blow out air. As you are coming to the end of your air supply, rise up to clear the water with your shoulders. Take a breath and drop down. Repeat several times about two seconds apart to practise the rhythm.

2. In your next drill, do as above, but now walk on the bottom of the pool submerged. Follow the same pattern as in your first drill. When you are comfortable doing these drills, combine your breathing practice with drills outlined in the kicking section.

Learning progression

The learning progression for the breaststroke is much like that of the freestyle. Remember that learning to swim should progress from easy to difficult tasks and from kicking to arm action.

1. The *body position* is similar to the freestyle, but instead of rolling from side to side, the body undulates as if you are attempting to ride the waves. The technique of this rolling action should be learned with kicking.

2. Practise your *kicking*, with and without the board, until you feel competent. Along with the kick, hip and ankle flexibility exercises must be done to keep the joints loose.

3. *Arm action* practice should begin only after the kick has been mastered. At the beginning, the arm pattern should be practised on deck and standing waist deep in the water.

4. Learn to *scull* right from the beginning of this stroke.

5. At first, swim short distances, without worrying about your breathing, so you can concentrate on your arm and leg technique. Then, introduce *breathing*, again beginning with short distances and gradually increasing the distance.

The breaststroke start

As with any racing start, you must react quickly and forcefully to make a speedy entry into the water. For the breaststroke, the entry needs to be deeper than usual, so you can use the underwater pull-out stroke.

The grab-start technique

The actual mechanics of the start and the procedure are exactly the same as in the freestyle. Dive off the block a little higher than usual so you will go deeper into the water. Once you level out under water, keep your body in a long, streamlined position to start the underwater pull-out stroke.

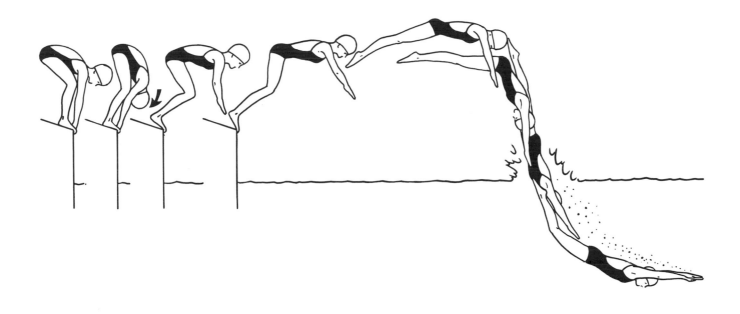

Fig. 2.10.   Breaststroke grab start technique.

The underwater pull-out stroke

Serious competitive swimmers always perform the underwater pull-out stroke to speed up the breaststroke at the start of a race and during turns. The breaststroke sequence usually starts with the arm action. After the starting dive, the swimmer doing the underwater pull-out stroke will come near the surface before the next stroke is taken. To maintain the speed generated by the dive, the underwater pull-out stroke was developed so that the swimmer can use the speed of the dive before coming to the surface.

To practise the pull-out stroke, push off the wall underwater into a full stretch and glide until you begin to lose speed. The same full stretch and glide should be done after the dive entry.

Your arms scull outward as they would at the start of a regular arm stroke with the same hand position, but not quite as wide. Bend your elbows when your hands reverse direction and move your hands in toward the mid-line of your body, with the thumbs leading under your chest. Keep your elbows pointing outward in line with your shoulders. Then forcefully move your whole arm backward, elbows moving to the side of your body and lower arms and hands extending along your thighs. Glide head first in a streamlined position until you feel yourself losing speed again.

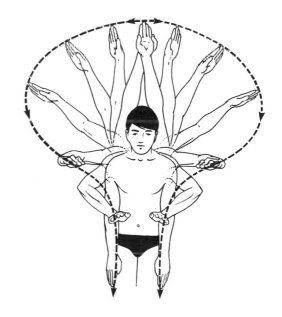

Fig. 2.11.   Underwater pull-out stroke arm path.

Fig. 2.12. Underwater pull-out stroke recovery arm path.

Begin the recovery arm movement by sneaking your hands and arms tight against the underside of your body to the arms-stretched-forward position. As your arms pass your stomach, bend your knees and lift your heels toward your buttocks to start the recovery action of your legs, and continue into a kick. The arm stretch and kick will move you closer to the surface helped by a slight elevation of your head.

Keep your head slightly raised so you can look over your arms and help the process. You can begin the first arm stroke before your head breaks the surface. In fact, this stroke will be the one that brings you to the surface as you begin the normal breaststroke.

> *Learning tip*
> Keep your body long and parallel with the surface, so you can stay under water long enough to complete the pull-out stroke.

> *Points to remember about the breaststroke start*
>
> • Do not rush your dive: you need good elevation from the diving block.
> • Allow your body to slide deeper into the water for the underwater pull-out stroke.
> • Streamline your body as you enter the water to cut down on resistance so the speed generated from the start is maintained.

Drills

1. When you have mastered the pull-out stroke, practise it across the width of the pool so you can use the lane lines to measure your distance. Because the lines on the bottom of the pool are at regular intervals you can establish your distance and the timing of each phase of the pull-out stroke. After taking a big breath, push off the wall at a depth of about half your height. See how far you can glide before you start to rise in the water. When you are passing over the second or third line (depending on how tall you are and how powerfully you pushed off), add the arm action to get you to the next line, gliding again without changing depth. Add the kick after you have passed the next line.

> *Learning tip*
> Always keep your body streamlined and don't rush the phases of the action. Be patient and allow your body to glide.

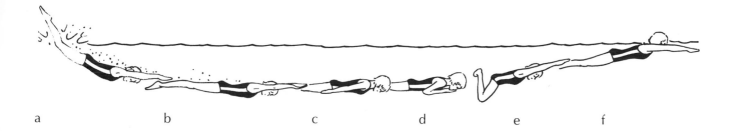

a   b   c   d   e   f

Fig. 2.13. Breaststroke underwater pull-out sequence from dive.

> *Learning tip*
> Learn the length of each phase by counting until you have developed a feel for your speed and distance.

The breaststroke turn

The breaststroke turn is governed by special rules. The rules for the turn are:

1. Both hands must touch the wall at the *same time* within one hand length of one another, either above or below the water-line. The important thing to remember is that both hands *must* touch.

2. Your shoulders must be parallel to the surface of the water until the touch is made. In other words, you cannot begin to turn until you have touched the wall.

3. When your legs are pushing off, you must turn onto your front as quickly as possible. Your shoulders must be horizontal when your feet leave the wall.

4. You can perform the pull-out stroke under water and begin the next regular stroke. But when your hands start the in-scull phase of the second arm stroke, your head must break the surface.

To do the turn as quickly as possible, the moment that your hands touch the wall, either on the same level or within a hand length of each other, quickly move one arm behind your back over the water with the elbow bent to start your body's spin. Pull your knees up under your body as you swing your legs toward the wall. The lead arm, now tucked behind your back, is ready to stretch forward as you complete your spin. The hand that is still

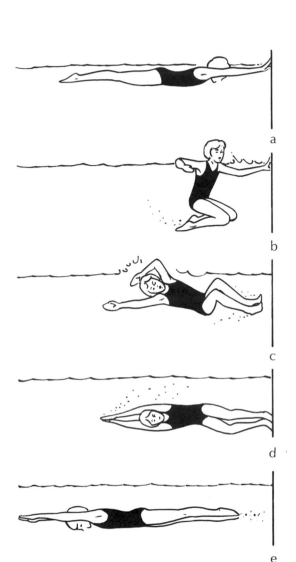

Fig. 2.14. Breaststroke turn.

touching the wall will push away, as your lead hand behind your back begins to stretch out.

Put your feet on the wall sideways, so you can easily roll onto your front by the time your feet leave the wall. As you place your feet on the wall, take a deep breath and drop your head and body under the water. Drop, do not dive, well below the surface. Make sure you are deep enough to complete the pull-out stroke. As you submerge, your hand will leave the wall and re-enter the water, moving forward to enter the water near your head.

> *Learning tip*
> Practise the turn in both directions to avoid developing bad habits from familiarity.

> *Learning tip*
> Take a breath before you put your head under water to avoid rushing the pull-out stroke.

The push-off phase

As soon as your body is submerged, the push-off phase for the breaststroke begins. This is different from the comparable natural glide position in the freestyle stroke. Finish your spin under the water by rotating your body toward the front as you straighten your knees. Make sure your body is in a straight line before your feet leave the wall. Your arms are fully stretched, waiting for your body to leave the wall. Drive off the wall as hard as you can. As you leave the wall, you will be fully stretched out, ready for the underwater pull-out stroke. (See Figure 2.14, position e.)

> *Learning tip*
> To take the best advantage of your turn, jump away from the wall explosively.

Drills

1. Stand on the deck about three metres away from a wall. Walk to the wall while moving your arms in the normal breaststroke. Do the legal touch, spin around, place one foot on the wall, and push yourself away gently for a long gliding walk.

2. Repeat as above in waist deep water. After the touch, spin around and drop well below the surface so you can place both feet on the wall. Push out into a good glide and perform the pull-out stroke.

3. From a short distance, glide to the wall, do the legal touch, spin and drop below the surface. Place your feet on the wall, push off, do the pull-out stroke and a few strokes on the surface.

4. Swim to the wall from a short distance, practise the turn, pull-out stroke and surface swimming.

Points to remember about the breaststroke turn

- Always touch the wall with two hands.
- Do not lift your head high out of the water; it will slow down your turn.
- Always keep your shoulders level in the approach to the touch.
- Drop—don't dive—well below the surface to ensure the proper completion of the pull-out stroke.
- Line your body up well before your feet leave the wall.
- Always drive away from the wall very hard.

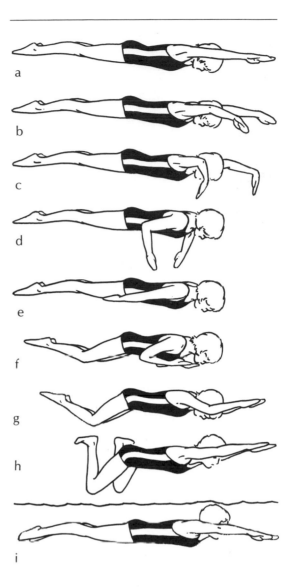

Fig. 2.15. Breaststroke underwater pull-out sequence.

3. THE BACKSTROKE

Alex talks about the backstroke

Swimming the backstroke is very demanding and takes a great amount of energy. It is ironic that the first national record I broke, at the age of nine, was in the backstroke. At that time, I felt the backstroke was technically my weakest stroke. Later, when I began to swim the individual medley, I found the backstroke to be the most tiring on my legs. I always tried to relax at the beginning of this stroke just to get accustomed to it.

When I was learning the backstroke, I had a problem with not rotating my body enough. I think this precipitated my shoulder injury. It is very important to make sure you roll your body in order not to put too much stress on your shoulder joints.

The kick is also very important in this stroke. Remember to use a good strong kick to keep the hips up and the body streamlined. A drill that helped me keep my hips up was kicking with my arms at my sides and my hands out of the water.

I have always felt that a major factor in successful backstroke competition is the turn. The turn is more crucial to this stroke than to the others, because you can't see the wall on the approach. It is important to watch for the flags to know how many strokes you need to get to the wall. The flags are there as a signal for the backstroke and can help you gain precious time. It may take a lot of practice to perfect the turn because you may be scared of hitting your head against the wall, but it is worthwhile.

FACTS ABOUT THE BACKSTROKE

The backstroke is often referred to as an upside-down freestyle stroke. As you practise the backstroke action, you will feel many similarities. But the backstroke is a more difficult stroke and demands a lot of energy. Being flipped over on your back is not just an unfamiliar body position. It also limits some of the movements that flow so easily in the freestyle.

The name "backstroke" can be misleading. Though backstroke rules state that you must always be on your back, in fact the stroke is performed more on the side of the body. Often beginning swimmers have a great deal of difficulty performing a smooth, co-ordinated action, because they try to stay strictly on their backs, not allowing sufficient body roll.

During the backstroke, you roll from side to side, as you do in the freestyle. According to backstroke rules, your body roll must be *less* than 90 degrees in relation to the surface of the water. So remember, even though the backstroke is performed with a side-to-side rolling motion, you must be careful not to roll right over onto your side.

In backstroke competition, a powerful start is essential.

MARCO CHIESA

The background

The ancestor of the modern backstroke is the "upside-down breaststroke". In this stroke, the swimmer was on the back using an over-the-head fanlike arm action and a breaststroke leg action. Some variation of this type of stroke was used in the 1904 Summer Olympic Games.

The rapid development of the front crawl greatly influenced the backstroke. At the 1912 Olympics, the backstroke became known as the "upside-down front crawl", with alternating arm action. But it wasn't until the 1948 Olympics that swimmers began to swim the backstroke we know today.

The action

The action in the backstroke is similar to the freestyle, except that it is performed on the back. Good backstroke technique provides a continuous motion through the water.

Your arms move alternately through the water, while your legs give six kicks to every arm cycle. Your armstrokes should be evenly timed to give you continuous and smooth motion. As in the freestyle, use your arms with strong kicking to move powerfully through the water.

To make sure that your body will not create unnecessary resistance, keep your body high in the water by letting your shoulders and head rest at the surface. The rhythmic rolling action of your shoulders also reduces the water resistance on your body.

Objectives for the backstroke

- Keep the smooth rolling motion of your body balanced by the continuous action of your legs.
- Keep your alternating arm action balanced for a continuous application of force against the water. As one hand and arm enters and catches the water, the other releases and rolls out of the water.

THE TECHNIQUE

Body Position

Good body position is essential to reduce drag and allow you to carry out the mechanics of your stroke. Basically you will be horizontal on your back, with minor deviations, and your body will rotate (less than 90 degrees) from side to side around the central axis, which runs from the top of your head through your torso.

The trunk position

Your body should be slightly bent at the hips to keep your hips just below the surface of the water and allow you to do a strong, deep kick. Your torso should slope upwards gently from your hips to your head so your chest is slightly above the surface of the water.

> **Learning tip**
> Do not sit down. Always keep your hips at the surface of the water and your chest "dry".

> **Learning tip**
> *Allow* the water to support your body instead of fighting for support.

The head position

The position of your head will affect, and in fact dictate, the position of both your torso and your legs. It is important to get used to the correct head position from the beginning. For the best head position, tilt your head up about 10 centimetres, as though the water were a cushion. This means your earlobes are just barely over the surface of the water and your chin is close to your chest. You should be able to watch your leg action.

> **Learning tip**
> Keep your head steady by imagining that you are balancing a glass of water on your forehead.

The leg position

If your head and torso are in the right position, the slight bend at your hips will automatically keep your thighs and knees just below the surface of the water. If they're not, adjust your head and torso positions and check again. Your feet should never come out of the water. (See Figure 3.1.)

> **Learning tip**
> Keep your legs stretched backward, as if you are trying to reach the opposite end of the pool.

> **Learning tip**
> When you practise your kicking drills, always be aware of your head and trunk positions.

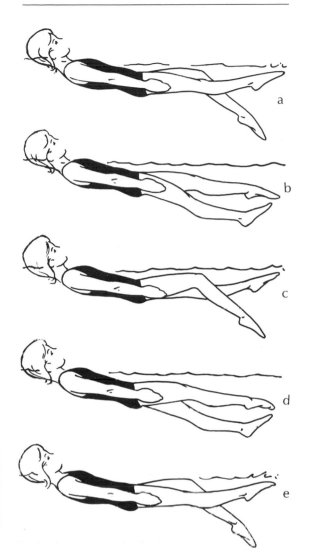

Fig. 3.1. Basic backstroke head and body position showing the kicking sequence.

> *Points to remember about the backstroke body position*
>
> - Don't allow your knees and feet to come above the surface of the water.
> - Keep your chest high and dry.
> - Keep your chin slightly tucked and look toward your feet.

Drills

Backstroke body position drills are best practised with the kicking action. You must always make sure that your kicking does not alter your basic body position. Your best body position kicking drill is illustrated in Figure 3.1.

Leg action

Move your legs continuously, alternating left and right, to maintain your body position and help with your speed. The kick should be learned and practised before you add the arm action, because good body position is so important for effective performance of this stroke. By learning the leg action first, you will develop a feel for where your body should be in the water and how your legs support you, before you begin to concentrate on providing speed with your arms.

The objective of the leg action is to control and support proper body position. It acts as a stabilizer as well as helping to maintain the speed generated by your arms.

The recovery phase

The following description of the leg action may make it sound as though the action is performed with your legs moving straight up and down in the water. In fact, your kick will follow the natural roll of your shoulders and your hips, and the kick strokes will be performed on slightly diagonal lines.

In the backstroke kick, the downward movement of your leg is really the recovery for the powerful upstroke, positioning your leg for the next kick. The action is started at your hip joint, leading with the back of your knee and keeping your leg straight. Your foot should start just below the surface of the water. It should be extended and turned slightly toward the middle. As your leg moves down, your foot should be loose at the ankle to allow the water to shape your foot for maximum resistance. As the downward moving leg gets below the knee level of the opposite, upward moving leg, your thigh stops moving downward.

However, by allowing your knee to bend, the downward movement of your lower leg continues and at the same time you forcefully extend your foot. This will force the water downward, trapped on the sole of your foot, to give a little more power to your kick. The downward movement of your foot will stop when it gets below the level of your buttocks. This usually takes place when the upward drive of the opposite foot is completed and the leg is fully extended. As your lower leg is completing its downward path, remember to slowly lift the knee of this leg upward to initiate the upward drive. This initial upward movement of the knee not only starts the drive phase of this leg, but also signals the other leg to start moving downward for recovery.

> *Learning tip*
> Move your feet up and down, as if they were fins without bony restrictions.

> *Learning tip*
> Always practise flexibility exercises for the joints in your legs and feet to improve your range of movement.

The drive phase

Moving from your hip joint, begin to move your lower leg upward, keeping your foot fully extended and turned slightly inward (pigeon-toed). Imagine that your shin is forcing the water up. Your foot will get into the action later. Stop your thigh and knee just below the surface and your foot will finish the kick in a whip-like motion, again just below the surface. This will create a mound of water rather than a big splash. At the completion of this kick, your foot will be fully extended and again pointed slightly inward.

> *Learning tip*
> When you kick, imagine your leg is an uncoiling bullwhip that speeds up as it snaps.

> *Learning tip*
> When you are finishing your kick, imagine that you are trying to touch your toes on the far end of the pool. Make sure you do a long stretch with your legs.

> *Points to remember about the backstroke leg action*
>
> * Never lift your knees or your toes out of the water.
> * Always finish the kick with "long legs".
> * Always kick hard. This will ensure a good body position and help to generate speed.
> * Always begin to move your legs from your hip joint.

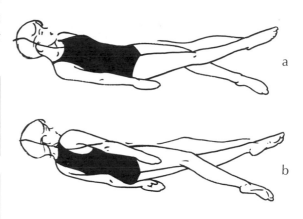

Fig. 3.2. Backstroke kicking with right-left body roll: (a) right roll; (b) left roll.

Fig. 3.3.   One arm up backstroke kicking drill.

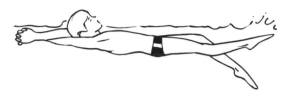

Fig. 3.4.   Two arms up backstroke kicking drill.

Drills

The similarity to the freestyle kicking makes learning the backstroke leg action easier. Make sure all kicking is done in the appropriate body position whenever possible.

1. Push off the wall into a back glide position with your arms at your side. Concentrate on kicking, while keeping your knees and feet under water. (See Figure 3.1.) This drill will also help you get a good feel for the proper hip and head positions.

   Because this drill does not involve any body roll, practise it again with shoulder and hip roll. But do this only after you are able to keep your knees and feet under water and have learned the feel for the appropriate body position.

2. This one-arm-up drill allows you to practise kicking in much the same body position as the complete stroke. Kick with one arm extended above your head in the water, while your other arm is resting along the side of your body. Make sure that the arm stretched above your head is straight, with your small finger in the water. Your body will be tilted to the side of the arm extended above your head. Switch arm positions at specified distances to get a feel for both sides of the roll.

3. For the two-arms-up drill, stretch both arms above your head, clasping your hands together and forcing your arms slightly below the level of your head and below the level of the water. This drill requires good shoulder flexibility. Without this flexibility, you will feel awkward and be unable to perform the drill with good body position. The limitation of this drill is that it does not allow any rolling action.

4. This drill is for advanced swimmers and uses progressively more difficult body positions as you build up your kicking strength. Kick for a predetermined distance, first with your arms folded across your stomach, then with arms folded across your shoulders. Then, with your arms under the water and at your sides, bend your elbows so you can stick your hands out of the water and point them at the ceiling. Next, lift your elbows to the surface of the water, fingers still pointing to the ceiling. Finally, continue kicking with your arms straight out of the water and pointing at the ceiling.

   The distance for each phase should be decided before you begin the drill. It is best to have longer distances for the first three phases and shorter distances for the last two. This drill is sometimes called "the submarine", because swimmers usually end up under water.

Arm action

As in the freestyle, the most effective arm action in the backstroke includes an up-and-down sculling motion with your hands.

Despite the alternating action of your arms, they must stay in the same relative position, like two spokes in a wheel. That is, as one arm enters the water, the other leaves it. The arm action in the backstroke is difficult to co-ordinate and it is better to master the movement pattern with one-arm drills before trying the continuous stroke with the appropriate shoulder and hip roll.

The objective of the arm action is to perform the alternating arm strokes smoothly and progressively faster. This provides continuously increasing speed, without disturbing the smooth rolling action of your body.

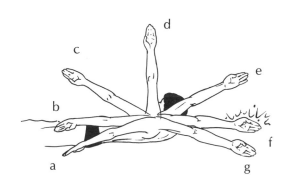

Fig. 3.5. Backstroke arm recovery sequence.

> *Learning tip*
> Always keep your body stretched out to get a high body position that will help the rolling action of your body.

The recovery phase

Your shoulder will come out of the water first, followed by the same side of your chest. When the stroke is correctly performed, your shoulder will rise out of the water automatically at the finish (while your opposite shoulder is dropping). This is because of the downward pressing action of your hand. As your shoulder moves up — in an upward and backward/forward shrug — it will actually raise your recovery arm out of the water with your hand leaving the water, little finger first, helped by your rising chest. At this point, you will be able to look along the length of your arm, as if you were sighting a gun. (See Figure 3.8, positions a, b.)

Your arms will leave the water perfectly straight and travel vertically through the air, re-entering the water behind and roughly in line with your shoulder. During this initial part of recovery, your body will be rolled away from the recovery arm to get your recovering shoulder high out of the water. As your recovery arm passes overhead, your shoulder will begin to lower back into the water, preparing for the eventual lift of the opposite shoulder.

> *Learning tip*
> When you are doing the backstroke, imagine that your body is a small boat in rough water, rolling from side-to-side, almost ready to tip over. This will help you to roll your shoulders. Your head stays straight and motionless.

The entry phase

Your arm should be straight as it enters the water, with your little finger entering first. As your arm enters the water, your shoulder will begin to roll into the water to allow a straight and deep entry. This roll will be helped by the opposite, finishing arm. The point

Fig. 3.6. Basic backstroke entry timing. (See Fig. 3.8., position k.)

of entry will be in line with and behind your shoulder. If you were lying on your back on a giant clock instead of in the water, the entry point of your left arm would be between 12 and 1, and your right arm would be between 11 and 12.

Your arm, still straight, will then continue its downward path until it reaches a depth of about 30 to 40 centimetres. It is important to realize that your arm is not only travelling downward, but also away from your head, increasing the planing action of your arm and hand. (See Figure 3.8, positions e,f,g.)

> *Learning tip*
> Keep your shoulder and chest high, so you can make an entry long and well beyond your shoulder.

The catch

The *catch* is in fact part of the power phase discussed below, since it sets up the speed of the stroke. The reason it is discussed separately is because it is more closely related to the entry phase.

Still straight, your arm continues moving down and begins to move a little sideways. At the desired depth, your hand should tilt a little to get into a better sculling position and move a few more centimetres out in order to catch the water.

The first power phase

When your hand has actually caught the water, your arm will start bending at your elbow in response to the force against your hand. This is the beginning of the first power phase of the stroke. Now your arm and hand will begin to scull outward and upward while your elbow points diagonally toward the pool bottom. In reality, only your lower arm and hand are moving, while your upper arm is maintaining a good diagonal stretch toward the pool bottom. Once your sculling hand rises above your elbow, your whole arm will move as a unit.

> *Learning tip*
> Think of your hand and lower arm as one paddle against the water.

The mid power phase

As the stroke reaches its mid peak, your elbow will continue to bend, as a result of the movement of the gradually insweeping and upsweeping hand. At this point, your arm will be bent about 90 degrees at your elbow, and your fingers will be about 15 centimetres below the surface but pointing toward it. Now your whole arm can begin the extension part of the stroke, starting at your shoulder. Because your hand and lower arm are accelerating faster

Fig. 3.7. (A) Backstroke underwater arm sequence, and (B) mid-stroke relative arm position (corresponds to position d).

than your upper arm, your hand will quickly take the lead in the movement.

> *Learning tip*
> During the underwater action, imagine your hand and arm as an accelerating propeller, constantly speeding up until it reaches your hip.

The final power phase

Your hand will now sweep inward and downward as your upper arm rotates toward your body. Your hand is constantly accelerating during this inward-downward movement. As your hand sculls, gradually rotate your hand until the palm faces down. By the end of the sweep, rotate your hand slightly away from your thigh. Your hand will literally drive or throw the water toward your feet and the bottom of the pool. This quick and forceful action will help your shoulder rise above the water and initiate your body roll. At the end of the phase, your arm will be straight and at the side of

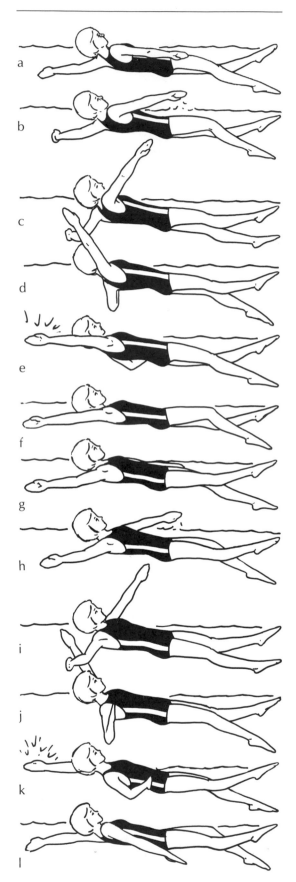

Fig. 3.8. Backstroke sequence.

your body with your hand below your buttocks. Your arm is now ready for the recovery.

Learning tip

During the arm action, think of your hands as the tips of big pencils drawing large "S"s. When you do a proper arm stroke, the path of your hand should describe the outline of a large "S".

Timing your arms and legs

Because you are on your back and limited in your movement by your shoulder joint, balanced timing is essential for effective stroke performance.

The timing of your leg movements is similar to that in the freestyle stroke. It follows a natural rhythm. Your right leg kicks up as your right arm enters and catches. Your left leg kicks up during the mid phase of the arm action. Your right leg kicks up again, as the right arm is extending into its final scull.

The timing of your arms requires a little more concentration. As your left arm enters the water, your right arm is just finishing its final downward scull (both arms are under water). (See Figure 3.8 position e.) As your finishing right arm releases the water resistance in preparation for the recovery, your left arm will be catching the water resistance at the opposite end of your body. This timing makes sure that your arms are continuously engaging water resistance for maximum movement through the water. Don't forget that your entry arm will be moving faster into the water, than your finishing arm will be completing its last movement.

Points to remember about the backstroke arm action

- Keep your arms straight during recovery and entry.
- Your hand should always enter the water as directly behind your shoulder as possible.
- Your hand must enter the water with your little finger first.
- Keep your arms moving faster and faster, as they go through their stroke pattern.
- Remember to draw a big "S" with your moving hands.
- Finish the stroke with a powerful snap of your hands below your thigh.
- Time the finish of one hand with the catch of the other.

Drills

1. Lie on the pool deck with both of your arms at your sides. Raise one arm vertically, reaching for the ceiling and then

lower your arm, as you would in the backstroke entry, to the deck. Remember to keep your arm straight. Your arm should end up beside your head, with your hand turned away from your head and your little finger touching the deck. This drill will help you feel the entry position. Close your eyes to get a better feel for the movement. Practise using one arm at a time, or as one arm goes to enter, lift the other back to the starting point. The limitation of this drill is that it does not allow your body to roll.

2. Stand with your back to the wall, about 30 to 40 centimetres away from it, and have someone guide your arm through its proper stroke path. This drill will allow body rotation, so your arms can reach the desired depth. At the same time, you will be able to check the position and movement of your hand. Once you have a feel for the movement, you can practise without help. Try doing this drill in front of a mirror to check your movements from time to time.

3. This is a one-arm drill in water. Start with the kicking drill, your arms at your sides. Recover one arm and go through the stroke path, maintaining a continuous and strong kicking action. This drill allows your body to roll, but because you don't have the benefit of the opposite arm's finishing hand to balance the roll, you must deliberately emphasize your shoulder movement. This drill is particularly good because you can focus on one arm at a time, while continuing to build strong kicking skills.

   Variations on this drill are limitless: change arms each length; change arms after four, three or two consecutive one-arm strokes; one arm for one length and then two arms for the next length and switch to one arm again; four strokes on each arm, then three, then two, then regular continuous; and so on.

4. This is a two-arm drill. The stroke is the same as in the regular backstroke; however, the arms move at the same time. Keep your arms straight during both the recovery and entry. You will bend your elbows sooner than in the regular stroke, because your arms are limited at the shoulder joint and a deep entry is inhibited. The double-arm drill stroke is shallower than the regular backstroke arm stroke. This drill will enhance the flexibility of your shoulders—the entry must be long and forceful—as well as emphasize the finishing sculling drive. Strong kicking is essential. Again, there is a disadvantage because this drill does not allow any shoulder roll. It should be followed by a drill that allows shoulder roll before you swim a backstroke set.

Breathing
Although you are on your back, and free to breathe at any time,

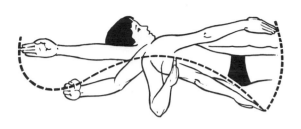

Fig. 3.9. "S" pattern of backstroke arm action.

it is best if you develop a definite breathing rhythm. If your breathing is not rhythmic, it may prevent a balanced stroke performance. Always breathe either when you begin to recover the right arm or when you recover the left arm.

Breathe in as your recovery arm is leaving the water. If you delay the breath, water may fall into your open mouth as your recovery arm passes overhead. Breathe out when the recovery arm is entering and the opposite arm begins its recovery. You may inhale on every arm recovery. If this is too frequent, try breathing on every second or third arm recovery.

Learning tip
Take a normal breath without opening your mouth too wide.

Points to remember about backstroke breathing

- Be regular and rhythmic in your breathing.
- Keep your head straight and do not turn your face to avoid water.
- Breathe out when your recovering arm enters the water. Breathe in when the arm leaves the water.

Drills
No breathing drills are needed for the backstroke, since your face will be out of the water.

Learning progression
Use the same principles that you followed for the breaststroke.

1. Spend time establishing a correct and strong *kicking action* and always be aware of the correct body position.

2. During kicking, always practise the *rolling action*. Some kicking drills are not entirely suitable for rolling. Make sure you regularly practise the ones that are.

3. When your kick is strong, *the one-arm stroke drill* is the next step. This drill should be practised with many variations and always with body roll.

4. Practise the path of the *arm stroke* in front of a mirror to see the muscles' action as your arms go through their pattern.

5. When you start to practise the *alternating arms stroke*, always swim short distances (five to six stroke cycles) for good control of the kick and body roll.

The backstroke start
The backstroke is started in the water. The rules state that in the ready position your toes must be under the surface of the water.

Usually your feet are side-by-side. However, when the end wall or the touch pad is slippery, most swimmers stagger their feet, with one lower than the other, for a stable push-off.

The objective of a good start is to jump away from the starting wall powerfully, and to quickly assume the proper body position and begin kicking before you start the arm strokes.

The start technique
Your initial position in the water is defined by the rules. Your toes are under the water. You must grip the starting bar(s), usually with your hands the width of your shoulders apart. On the command "take your mark", bend your elbows to pull your body up so your head is bent over and close to your chest. Tuck your chin toward your chest. Bend your knees to help support the start position. You will be in a position similar to a coiled-up rattlesnake, ready to spring out and strike.

> *Learning tip*
> Take up the starting position so that your hips are just at the surface of the water.

At the sound of the gun, spring away from the wall by throwing your head back and extending your arms with a final push of your hands. Bring your hands back, swinging around the side, to the front of your head. Your arms should be either straight or bent at the elbows, but close to and parallel to the surface of the water. At the same time, straighten your legs to drive yourself away from the wall. Just after your feet leave the wall, your body should be fully stretched over the water with your arms tight against and stretched beyond your head. Your head will be slightly tilted toward the water, ready for entry.

> *Learning tip*
> Think of jumping away from the wall, rather than just pushing against the wall.

> *Learning tip*
> Try to splash some water back to the starting block with your feet to achieve a high kick leg position.

As your body begins to enter the water — hands first — your feet will be above the water. Lift your head a little as it submerges, squeezing your arms against your ears, to help level your body as it slips through the "hole" created by your hands and head. (At this point, your feet will be higher than your head.) Maintain a stretched and streamlined body throughout the entry.

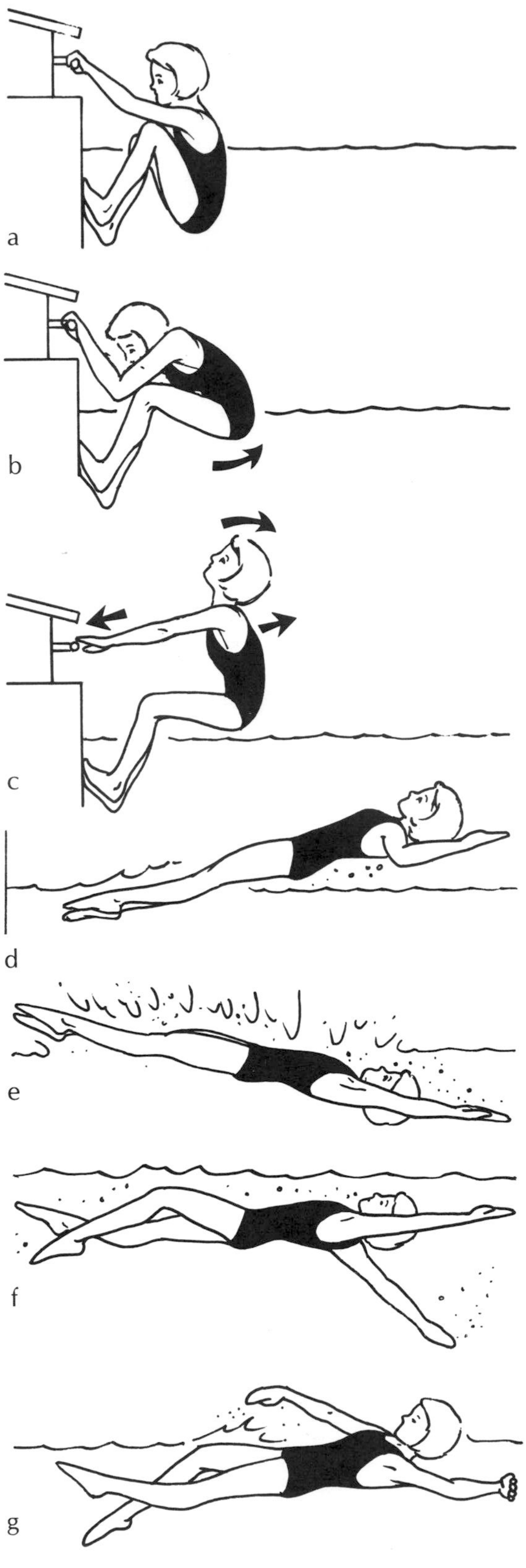

Fig. 3.10. Backstroke start sequence: (a) ready position; (b) take your mark; (c, d) flight; (e) entry; (f, g) swim out.

Learning tip
While you're in flight, stretch away from the wall as though you were trying to touch the other end of the pool.

After entry, glide a little and then begin to kick as you feel yourself slowing down, at about four to five metres from the wall. Almost immediately after you begin to kick, tilt your head up a little for proper position and take the first arm stroke. This arm stroke will bring your body to the surface. As the opposite hand begins to break the surface, it will go into the second arm stroke while your initial arm is now ready to recover.

Points to remember about the backstroke start

- Test your feet on the wall to find out how slippery the wall or touch pad is before you place your feet for the start.
- Lift your hips over the water as you drive away from the wall.
- Remember to take a breath as your body is stretched over the water.
- Stretch to make your body feel like a slim torpedo.
- Start your kicking as soon as your body is completely submerged.
- Get back to the surface with the first arm stroke, initiated immediately after you begin kicking.

Drills

1. Practise jumping on the deck from a half-squat position with your arms held over and against your head. This will simulate the body position after the grip bar has been released and give you an idea of the power required to propel your body away from the wall. Do this drill on a dry surface to avoid slipping and hurting yourself.

2. Assume the starting position in the deep end of the pool by hanging on to the lip of the pool. On your own command, jump away from the wall as far as you can and stay flat. Try to stay very close to the surface. Do not attempt to kick your legs up. Just practise a flat glide away from the wall for distance. End each glide by getting into a streamlined position and kicking as your body slows down.

3. To learn the up-kick from the wall, squat-stand in the gutter at the edge of the pool (a roll-out gutter is the best) and jump away from the wall, making sure that your jump is flat. Because your feet are above the water at the start of the jump and your head will naturally go back and down, it will be easy to maintain a high leg position with minimal effort. It is important to

fall back and not stand up in order to achieve a flat, long drive away from the wall. At the moment of entry, your head should be tilted up to stop the downward movement of your body, making sure that you are not wasting time by going too deep.

4. The next drill is to practise at the starting block with the starting bar, going through the above steps. A well executed backstroke start should surface a good distance beyond the turn-indicating flags.

The backstroke turn

As with the other turns, the backstroke turn is also governed by specific rules. You must touch the wall with the foremost part of your body (hand, head, shoulder, elbow). You must be more on your back, than on your stomach, and never pass the vertical when you touch the wall. You must also be on your back when you push off.

There are several varieties of turns that are effective. Practise and select the one that suits your body type. Three different turns will be presented. Each turn is distinguished by how the head-toe reverse is done. Each requires a particular level of experience and expertise. Learn all three, so you can choose the appropriate one for a particular race.

> *Learning tip*
> Practise turns with both hands to develop your confidence.

To help you anticipate the turn and estimate when you will touch the wall, a backstroke turn flag rope is suspended over the water exactly five metres from the wall. When your head is under the flags, you can tell exactly when your hand will touch the wall by counting the number of arm strokes it takes you to cover the distance. Once you learn the count, the rhythm of your stroke will be kept up and you can transfer your speed smoothly into a quick turn and push-off.

> *Learning tip*
> Always count from the turning flags and learn to adjust according to the relationship of your head to the flags (in front or beyond) as you start counting.

Your objectives in practising the turns will be to maintain the speed you have when you approach the wall during the turn. Leave the wall with such force that the turn will increase your speed.

> *Learning tip*
> Always stretch your body long, while approaching the wall for the turn, to allow for continuity in kicking.

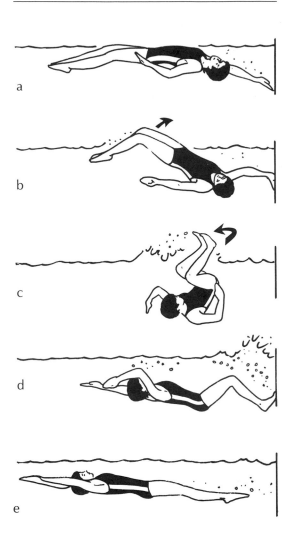

Fig. 3.11. Backstroke flip-pivot turn.

The flip-pivot turn technique

This turn is called the flip-pivot turn because, when your legs are higher than your head, you *flip* as you reverse direction. Because you are sliding on your back, you also *pivot*.

During your last arm recovery before the turn, move your arm behind your head and flex your wrist so your hand will touch the wall about 30 to 45 centimetres under water. Place your hand on the wall, with your fingers pointing toward the bottom of the pool. Your opposite arm should be at your side.

Following your hand, your head and shoulders will submerge and allow your legs and hips to rise. As your hand touches, move your head away from the touching arm's shoulder toward the opposite shoulder. Bend your elbow slightly to absorb and redirect your speed as your hand presses against the wall. Remember that in order to initiate your body's flip-pivot action in this turn, the move of your head and the pressure on the wall must be synchronized.

Your knees will be elevated because you dropped your head, and should now move *toward* the touching arm on the wall to lead the pivoting action. Your feet will trail behind and over the surface of the water. The lifting action of your knees and the low head position will make your body rotate in a circle-like manner. This is the flip part of the turn.

As you move your head and press on the wall, the pivoting action will begin. It will continue as your legs rise and swing around over the water to the wall. Your opposite arm should be brought in a sculling motion, up to your head, where the touching arm will join it. Slide around on your back, like a record on a turntable, then reach for the wall with your feet to avoid making a complete circle with your body. This is the pivot part of your turn.

You are now pivoting on your back, parallel to the surface of the water, with the arm that was on the wall moving to your head. Your feet will touch the wall at approximately the same spot where your hand touched. At the moment your feet are firmly on the wall, your knees should be bent to not quite 90 degrees and your toes are pointing to the surface. Extend your arms beside your head, covering your ears. Your legs can now begin their powerful drive from the wall.

This push off the wall puts your body into a stretched and streamlined position. Almost immediately after your feet leave the wall, begin your kicking drive once again. At this point, your chin may be slightly tucked to your chest as you prepare to surface. From this point, follow the same procedure you use during a start.

> *Learning tip*
> Always pivot in the direction of your arm that is on the wall.

The open-bucket turn

This turn is similar in approach and push-off to the flip-pivot turn. However, both your hand placement and the push-off will be shallower. This turn can be used effectively in the 200 metre backstroke and in the individual medley. It allows one breath during the turn.

The approach is as described in the flip-pivot turn. Place your hand on the wall about 20 centimetres deep. Your shoulders and head will not go under the water when you touch. When the touch is made, your head will be slightly elevated by moving away from the touching arm's shoulder. Your knees will be elevated as they were in the flip-pivot turn. Take one breath as your feet swing around to the wall, clear of the water, then drop under water to the level of your feet. The push off the wall is again swift. It is shallower and shorter than the flip-pivot, but possesses the same streamlined efficiency.

The roll-over turn

This turn is for experienced swimmers because it requires a great deal of control to avoid disqualification. It appears to be a more natural action than the other turns, puts less strain on your shoulders and can be performed more quickly.

As you approach the wall, the recovering arm, instead of approaching the wall behind its shoulder, will approach the wall by moving across your face. As your arm nears your face, turn your head slightly away from your approaching arm. This action will rotate your body to bring your recovering arm's shoulder close to the surface of the water. At the moment of the touch, make sure your upper shoulder has not gone beyond the vertical and make sure you are still on your back.

Place your hand on the wall a little deeper than the 30 to 40 centimetres of the flip-pivot turn to accommodate the somersault

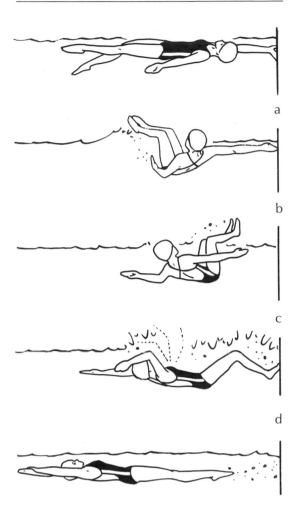

a

b

c

d

Fig. 3.12. Backstroke open-bucket turn.

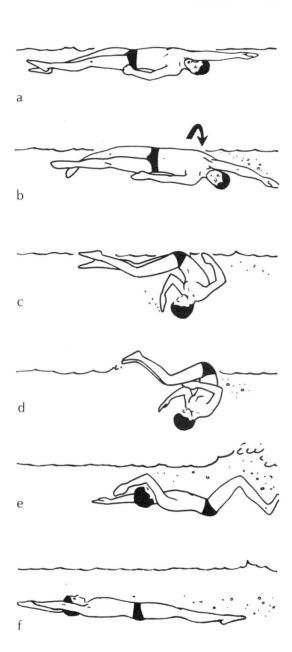

a

b

c

d

e

f

Fig. 3.13. Backstroke roll-over turn.

portion of the turn. After the touch is made, you will continue to roll and twist onto your back with your chin tucked to your chest, assuming a body position similar to that of the middle of a somersault. The push from the wall will be deep and requires a strong kick to bring you back up to the surface. The underwater portion of this turn is longer than in the others. Many swimmers find that the dolphin kick is better for this turn, until the first arm stroke is begun. In fact, many swimmers use the dolphin kick at the start of the race as well, especially if the start is deeper than about one metre. The position of your head must be closely controlled throughout this turn to avoid too much time under water.

Points to remember about the backstroke turns

- Always approach the wall with strong kicking.
- Allow your head and shoulders to go under water with the last stroke (except in the open-bucket turn), so that your hips and knees will rise easily.
- Never move your head down to initiate the pivot. Always move it away from the supporting shoulder.
- Never kick your feet up in the air as you lift them out of the water. Keep your feet close to the level of the water for a quick transfer to the wall.
- Drive away from the wall the instant your feet are firmly planted on the wall.
- Push into a stretched and streamlined body position and start your kicking immediately after leaving the wall.

Drills

It is extremely important to practise the turn drills using both arms. The following drills assume that the flip-pivot turn is learned first.

1. Practise the turning action on the pool deck while lying on a plastic mat about an arm's length from a wall. The mat should be wet to allow a frictionless pivot. Place your hand on the wall, fingers pointing down, arms straight. Move your head away from the shoulder of the touching arm. At the same time, lift your knees and push away from the wall with your hand. These combined movements will make your body pivot around on your back, so your feet will be at the wall. Place your feet on the wall and push away from the wall. At the same time, stretch your arms along your head to cover your ears and extend into an imaginary glide position. Then practise with someone who can help you to pivot more easily.

    The limitation of this drill is that your head and shoulders cannot be dropped as they would be in the water.

2. Practise the above drill in the water, without the approach.

3. In the water, kick hard to the wall from about five metres away, with one arm extended in front of your head. Keep your arm straight and against your head, with your little finger in the water. As your hand is about to touch the wall, rotate it to allow your palm to be placed on the wall, fingers pointing down. Your kicking should continue, as your hand is placed on the wall, with your head under water to emphasize the importance of kicking right into the wall. Allow your hips to rise.

   At the next stage, try a similar approach. But this time move your head away from the touching arm's shoulder and allow your knees to rise out of the water in response to the reversal of the force generated by your kick. Your shoulders will also be allowed to dip under the water with your head.

   As you progress with this drill, do the turn and push-off, with your arms extended over and in front of your head, and kick hard. Remember to push away from the wall with your supporting arm at the instant your head moves away from your shoulder.

4. Swim in toward the wall with one arm. Perhaps two strokes from the wall, stop your arm movement and kick only. Execute the turn and kick out hard in a perfectly streamlined body position. Repeat drill with opposite arm.

5. Swim in with the full stroke from about 10 metres away. Under the backstroke turn flag, start counting to five arm movements. On the fifth, stop stroking and continue with the kick only to the wall, execute the turn and kick out hard. Most young swimmers require about five strokes from the flags to get to the wall. With practice and experimentation, you will be able to approach the wall with confidence.

6. Swim in, turn and swim out, emphasizing kicking and stream-lining. The first stroke after your turn should be taken when your head is under the flags. As you push off the wall and your kicking becomes stronger, the distance to the flags will be covered more quickly.

4. THE BUTTERFLY

Alex talks about the butterfly

The butterfly, properly executed, is a very beautiful stroke to watch, because of its flowing rhythm. However, if it is not done correctly, it can be the most awkward and painful stroke to watch. From the swimmer's point of view, it is a very difficult stroke to learn. It took me many years to perfect it.

One tip my coach gave me to help me remember the proper technique was to trace a keyhole pattern with my hands during the pull. It is also essential to keep your hips up, to maintain the flowing action of the stroke.

The greatest challenge in doing the butterfly stroke is to keep an even rhythm. The undulating motion must be perfectly timed. Just remember to be fluid in the water, like a dolphin swimming in the ocean. One drill that helped me to acquire the rhythm needed for the butterfly was the one-arm drill. Because this drill overemphasizes the undulating motion, it helped me to get the flow of the stroke.

FACTS ABOUT THE BUTTERFLY STROKE

The butterfly looks deceptively simple and many swimmers mistakenly rush through the learning and training progressions for the stroke without mastering the fundamentals. Because of this, the "fly", as it is commonly known, has a frightening reputation among swimming students. Although the butterfly relies more on kicking support than any of the other competitive strokes, it can be learned and practised progressively, just as the freestyle, the breaststroke and the backstroke can.

The butterfly is also sometimes referred to as the "dolphin", because the kicking action resembles the movements of a dolphin's tail. Try to visualize a dolphin's tail and then picture how your legs can duplicate that effect. The idea is to move like a dolphin, undulating up and down, in and out of the water. The kick, which is very important in this stroke, is done twice for every arm stroke.

The background

The butterfly stroke is the result of the impatience of swimmers and coaches with the relatively slow breaststroke. In the late 1920s, swimmers began to experiment with recovering the arms over the water. This new over-the-water arm recovery gained such rapid popularity that for a time the conventional breaststroke became an almost extinct competitive event at major international meets.

The leg action of the butterfly remained the same as in the breaststroke for many years. But it changed when swimmers with poor breaststroke kicks began to experiment with vertical dipping

The butterfly may be the most graceful stroke.

MARCO CHIESA

movements of the legs. This eventually developed into the dolphin leg action now in use.

The official butterfly stroke, as it is known today, was first performed at the 1956 Summer Olympic Games.

The action

In the butterfly, arms and legs stroke together so that for every arm cycle two kicks are performed. The kicks usually pick up the slack at the end and the beginning of the arm stroke, to provide the free flowing continuity of the stroke.

Good butterfly technique gives the impression that the swimmer is gently gliding up and down with the flow of the waves. The underwater arm stroke follows the pattern of an old-fashioned keyhole or an hourglass figure. The legs follow the up-and-down rhythmical pattern of a giant dolphin tail. Most of the power in the butterfly stroke is generated by the arms, but the contribution of two powerful kicks makes the arm stroke even stronger.

Like the other strokes, the butterfly is governed by specific rules that restrict your movements. Your arms must recover over the water. At the same time, your shoulders must stay parallel to the water surface. Your legs must also move together, as though they were one big fin.

Although the body is undulating up and down, it is important to maintain a streamlined position close to the surface to reduce the resistance of the water against the body.

Objectives for the butterfly stroke

- Keep your body undulating, smoothly and rhythmically, as if you are imitating a dolphin.
- Time your kick and the finish of your arm stroke, so that your body moves over the water without losing much speed.

THE TECHNIQUE

Body position

Unlike the other strokes where you are trying to establish a stable body position, in the butterfly your body position is constantly changing. The dynamic nature of the body during the butterfly creates many different body positions. Rather than dividing this section into "The trunk position", "The head position", etc., it makes more sense to describe the action and note how the body conforms to it.

In the butterfly stroke, you will be continually moving your shoulders and your hips up and down as you travel through the water. It is best to start out by moving your hips up and down a great deal. Less experienced swimmers may exaggerate the hip undulation. But as you progress with the stroke and gain confidence, your body's undulation will become smoother.

> *Learning tip*
> Practise proper body position by picturing yourself as an eel, a snake or a dolphin slipping through the water, bending without restriction. (See Figures 4.1 and 4.2.)

> *Learning tip*
> Your head and shoulders always move as one unit, just as your legs do.

> *Points to remember about the butterfly body position*
>
> • Keep your hips loose, so your buttocks can move up and down in reaction to the leg action.
> • Always look forward, so your undulation is controlled and you are able to streamline the body whenever possible.
> • Keep your head and shoulders moving as one unit.

Drills

1. Stand straight on the pool deck, with your feet together and your arms stretched over your head. Bend forward and then backward about 30 to 40 centimetres from your waist, keeping your arms over your ears and your knees straight. Imitate the way trees move in the wind. Also, try this drill with your arms at your sides.

2. Lie on your hips across a bench, with your arms and legs stretched out. Bend up and down rhythmically. This is a good drill because you are now close to the body position you will assume in the water.

3. Try drill number two on your stomach in the water. It is important to remember that, as you learn the kicking action, the undulation or movement of your body will improve automatically.

Leg action

Your legs kick together at the same time in their up and down movement. You are not allowed to do alternate kicking as in the freestyle. The current rules state that your feet must stay together at all times. Your goal, when you are kicking your legs, is to create speed and help maintain your stroke rhythm.

As in the backstroke and the freestyle, your leg action will originate from your hips. Remember that for every arm cycle, two complete kicks are performed.

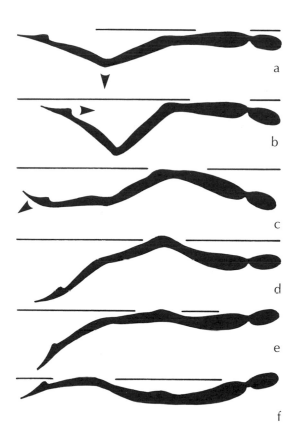

Fig. 4.1.   Butterfly leg action. Note fluctuating body position.

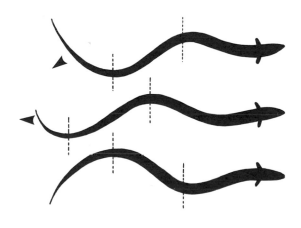

Fig. 4.2.   Eel swimming with whip action.

Learning tip
If you have seen a dolphin frolic in a swim tank, try to imitate one to develop a nice sliding-gliding and rhythmic butterfly stroke.

The recovery phase
At the bottom of your kick, your legs and feet will be fully stretched out. Begin moving your legs up, starting at the hip joint. Remember to keep your legs straight. Lift your legs up to the surface as if the backs of your knees were leading. Lower your hips at the same time to form a little arch in your back. (See Figure 4.1, position f.)

The drive phase
As in recovery, the initial movement, this time downward, starts from your hips as you allow your thighs to drop. Just as the recovery movement is led by the back of your knees, the downward movement of the drive is led by the front of your knees. (See Figure 4.1, position b.) For a well-groomed kick, your knees should be bent less than 90 degrees. But, in the beginning, it is better to have more bend in your knees, rather than less. In fact, you should bend them enough to allow your feet to just break the surface. This will ensure that you eventually develop the proper bend for a powerful kick.

Learning tip
Always bend your knees enough to allow them to lead the kicking action.

Once your feet have surfaced, your legs should begin to straighten, uncoiling like a bullwhip, as they progress through the downward movement. (See Figure 4.1, positions c, d.) Your feet begin to stretch out from your ankle joints as your legs uncoil in an attempt to force back the water that is trapped on your feet. Make sure that you keep your ankles and knees together.

Learning tip
Keep your legs and ankles loose, so you can *feel* the water.

As your legs progress through the drive, lift your hips to the surface so your swimsuit is visible above the water. Think of your legs, from your hips to your toes, as a teeter-totter. As one end goes up, the other end goes down. This downward, uncoiling action of your legs must be crisp and powerful, ensuring that your hips rise effortlessly as your feet complete their kick.

Fig. 4.3. Kicking at the wall.

Learning tip
Think of your legs as one unit to make sure your legs and feet stay together.

At the top of the recovery, your legs will pause for a moment to allow your body to slide forward in the water. At this point, your body will be stretched forward and streamlined to make sure you take advantage of the powerful drive of the kick.

Learning tip
Stretch your ankle joints daily to make sure your foot movements are loose and flexible.

Points to remember about the butterfly leg action

- Keep your ankles and knees together at all times.
- Accelerate the movement of your feet during the kick to ensure a strong whip action at the end.
- Allow your hips to rise as you complete your kick and stretch your chest forward to help achieve a good glide.

Drills

1. Hold on to the lip of the pool with one hand. Place the other on the wall, fingers pointing downward. Put your face in the water and begin kicking. Kick in short bursts, without breathing, in order to concentrate on the movement. This drill will help you practise the symmetrical and undulating kicking that is essential to the butterfly.

2. This drill is called "the armless dolphin". Push off from the bottom of the pool with your arms at your sides and your head level with your shoulders but aiming to surface with two or three kicks. Start kicking as soon your feet are off the bottom. Kick for short distances and without breathing. By keeping your arms at your sides, your body is really free to undulate in the water like a playful dolphin. As you establish a rhythm in your kicking, you can begin to practise taking a breath after a few kicks on the surface.

   As a variation on this drill, try it with one of your arms stretched over your head. Eventually, you can try kicking with both of your arms stretched forward.

   As a further variation, practise the drill under water, as if you were a dolphin. This variation has an additional advantage in that the water pressure, or the feeling of the water on your body, is the same all over, so you can get used to what feels

Fig. 4.4. Armless dolphin.

a

b

Fig. 4.5. Dolphining with and without a kickboard.

good and what does not feel quite right. You can begin practising the underwater dolphin drill on your front for fun and to help you learn better control. It should be practised on your sides as well.

3. This drill will help you feel how your body should move through the water. Lie on your back and kick with your arms at your sides. At first, your head and shoulders will be part of the undulating movement. As you get more experience and confidence, try to keep your head and shoulders at the surface.

As a variation on this drill, try it with your arms stretched over your head and you will be able to feel how your kick provides a surge of speed.

4. Practise kicking with a kickboard. This drill is an advanced drill. It requires a great deal of power and control for proper performance. For this reason, a kickboard should not be used until all other drills are performed properly and with confidence. You should also kick in this position without the board.

Arm action

Your arms also work as one unit. The rules state that you must recover both arms simultaneously, and that they must enter the water with shoulders lined up and parallel to the water's surface. Because both arms stroke and recover at the same time, the arm stroke is not designed to create a continuous force against the resistance of the water, as it is in the freestyle and the backstroke. This discontinuity may interrupt your rhythm, especially during the recovery phase, and you may lose some speed. In order to avoid this, it is important to perform the arm action with confidence and power. The correct timing of your kick in relation to your arm action will minimize your speed loss.

Your objectives, as you practise the arm action, are to keep the action symmetrical during both the recovery and the power phase. This will give you better control of your upper body and will generate a great surge of power.

The recovery phase

At the end of each stroke, your arms will be at your sides, loosely extended with your palms facing your thighs, ready to begin the recovery. Your body will be at its highest position—shoulders and elbows out of the water — and you will have finished taking a breath. (See Figure 4.11, position e.) Your arms should come out of the water almost straight, but relaxed, with your elbows slightly leading. The slight elbow elevation is important to avoid stiff arm recovery. Your hands will leave the water with the little fingers in the lead and be lifted high out of the water. Sweep your arms forward in a circular pattern, high over the water, to the point of entry in front of your shoulders. (The extent of your arm sweep will, of course, be determined by how flexible your shoulders are.)

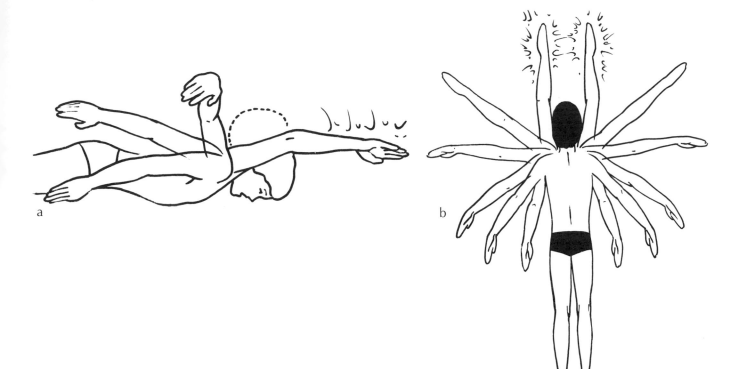

Fig. 4.6. Fly-arm recovery (a) side view, and (b) top view.

Your arms will be led forward by the backs of your hands until your arms are in line with your shoulders. Once you reach that point, rotate your arms inward and forward, first with your thumbs in the lead and then with the tips of your fingers leading. This rotation will give you a long forward reach. (See Figure 4.11, positions f, g, h.)

> *Learning tip*
> Finish your arm stroke just below the swimsuit line on your thighs, for a loose and controlled arm recovery.

> *Learning tip*
> Always lead the recovery with the back of your hands to ensure a circular arm path.

The entry phase
When your arms are ready to enter the water, they will be loosely stretched in front of your shoulders, hands turned outward and

slightly lower than your elbows. The backs of your hands will be facing each other, thumbs down. Your arms should be the width of your shoulders apart and stretched forward, just a bit higher than your head. At the moment your hands enter the water, your arms should stretch forward from your shoulders, not just from your elbows, with your wrists slightly flexed.

> *Learning tip*
> Always do a long stretch during entry to allow your hips to rise to the surface.

As your arms stretch forward and are about to begin their downward path, slide your chin forward to flatten your back and put your weight on your chest. Make sure that your hands are lined up with your lower arms at the moment of entry. This will keep your body streamlined and further reduce drag.

The catch

As your arms go under the water, they should start to scull out and slightly down. Your arms will move naturally because your elbows are still slightly elevated. During this movement, your torso will be sliding forward as if it's trying to pull away from the rest of you. When your hands have swept outside the width of your shoulders, change their pitch to move further downward, in position to begin their inward scull. This point represents the *catch*, the beginning of the power phase, and is similar to the catch phase in the breaststroke. (See Figure 4.7, positions a, b.)

The first power phase

The power phase is made up of several sweeping sculls that provide the speed in the stroke. It is also worth repeating that your arms should be constantly accelerating as they complete the stroke cycle.

The first out-scull of your arms has very little power. The power phase starts only after you've caught the water. As soon as your hands catch the water, begin to scull inward, bending your elbows and keeping them close to the surface. During this inward scull, make sure that your shoulders are still forward to keep your elbows up high and to keep them from moving. During the in-scull, it is your hands that are moving, not only inward but also up toward your chest, to make sure your elbows stay bent. They should be led by your thumbs, but it is important not to let them over-rotate and lose the water resistance you have just "caught". At the end of this phase, your hands will be close to each other and level with your neck, pointing diagonally toward each other. (See Figure 4.7, positions c, d.)

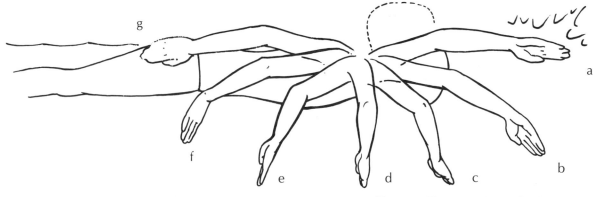

Fig. 4.7. Fly-arm action, side view.

Fig. 4.8. Fly-arm action (front view of Fig. 4.7., position (d).

> ### Learning tip
> To make sure that your elbows stay high, push your shoulders and your elbows forward so your hands and lower arms can move in the prescribed path.

The mid power phase
Once your hands are close and at neck level, they should begin an outward and backward scull, started by a slight inward leading move of your elbows. Make sure you keep your upper arms close to the surface, so your elbows will not drop during this slight movement and make your hands slip off the water. Your hands should aim at your hips during this outward scull, with fingers pointing to the bottom of the pool. They must also remain under your body during this phase.

> ### Learning tip
> Your arms must speed up as they progress along the stroke path. Think of your arms as a car at a stoplight. When the light changes, the car quickly accelerates until it gets to the next light, just as your arms should accelerate to the end of the cycle.

The final power phase
As your hands reach the level of your navel, they continue to scull out and then quickly scull in toward your hips. Meanwhile rotate your arms and keep your elbows high. Finish your hand movement with your fingers completely stretched to help your shoulders surge forward. At the same time, stretch your arms at the elbow until they are nearly straight. The palms of your hands will now be facing your thighs, little fingers up, ready to recover. Take care that your hands do not sweep above your hips.

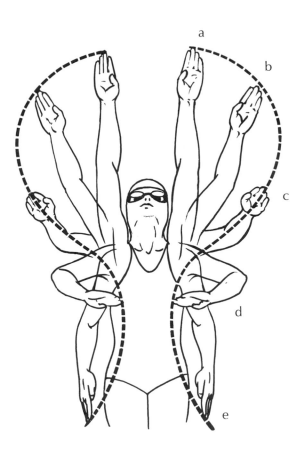

Fig. 4.9. Keyhole hand path, underneath view.

Timing of the arms and legs

Successful butterfly swimming relies on an easy flowing and rhythmical stroke. This is created by the proper timing of your arms and legs.

The relationship between the arm stroke and the kick is simple: for every arm stroke, kick twice. The two kicks are matched to a specific position in the arm stroke. The timing of the kicks is also related to the timing of your breathing.

The first kick is performed just as your arms enter the water (see Figure 4.11 position i). At this point, a breath has been taken and your head is under water so your hips will be high, above the level of your head and shoulders. As your arms scull out for the catch, complete the drive phase of your kick. Your legs will recover during the first and the mid power phases of the arm drive.

Take the second kick as your hands pass under your navel. This is also the point where you take a breath (see Figure 4.11 position e). Your head will come out of the water for a breath after your hands leave the chest area. Your second kick will be completed

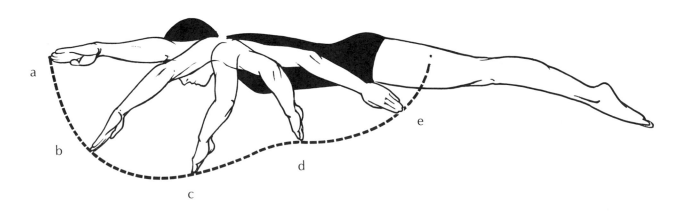

Fig. 4.10. Keyhole hand path, side view.

as your hands finish the final scull toward your thighs. Because your head and shoulders are up at this point, it is difficult to bring your hips up high as well, but do your best.

> *Learning tip*
> Do the first kick as your head goes down after your breath. Do the second kick as your head comes up to breathe.

> *Learning tip*
> To keep the proper rhythm and timing between your arms and legs, count in your mind, or say in your mind, KICK-PULL-KICK. Repeat this rhythm again and again.

Both kicks in the butterfly stroke should be equally strong. Traditionally, swimmers think that one of the kicks, usually the first, is stronger than the second. But an unequal distribution of effort will make your hips drop deeper and deeper and cause drag. It is especially important to keep this in mind as you learn the stroke.

> *Points to remember about the butterfly arm action*
>
> * Your hands should leave the water with your little finger in the lead.
> * Keep your arms long and relaxed during recovery.
> * Bring your arms over the water symmetrically, and have them enter the water thumb first.
> * After entry, don't begin your arm stroke immediately. Stretch forward while your legs are kicking down.
> * Always bend your elbows under the water for a more efficient stroke.
> * Keep your hands under your body as you go through the different phases of the arm action.
> * Finish your arm stroke with a powerful sculling snap of your wrists at the bottom line of your swimsuit.

Drills

The butterfly is a beautiful but unusual stroke that demands a lot of energy from the beginner. Because of this, it is best to start out swimming short distances, whether practising the regular stroke or some modified drill. Although these drills pertain to the arm action, you must also remember the other points you learned about the stroke.

1. Stand in front of a wall with your arms extended over your head and draw the shape of the stroke path on the wall — the

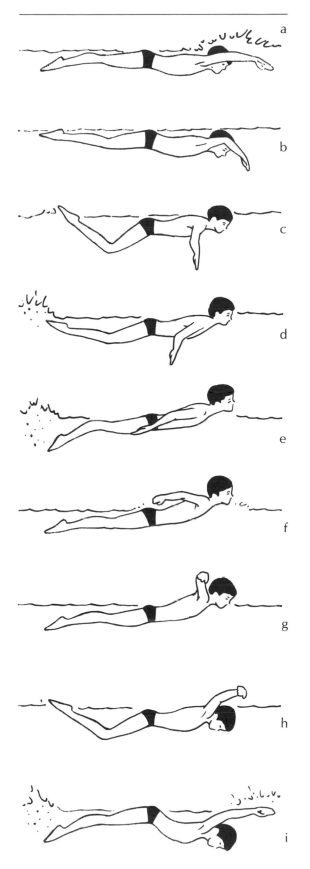

Fig. 4.11. Fly stroke cycle.

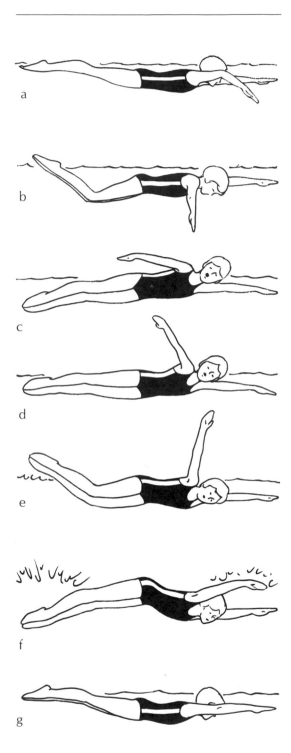

Fig. 4.12. One-arm fly drill with rest arm forward.

hourglass figure. (See Figure 4.9.) Make sure to keep your elbows in position. This drill allows you to both visualize and feel the movement pattern and learn how to control the moves of your arm before you get into the water.

2. Stand in an open, dry space clear of any object, with your hands close together and under your chin, and your elbows sticking out to the side, in line with your shoulders. Drive your hands down in front of your chest, bringing your elbows to your sides. As your hands are performing the final sculling flick, jump up off the floor as if your body is responding to the force of the arm stroke. Practise this drill to teach yourself the importance of speeding up your arms as they move through the stroke.

3. Perform drill number two in modified form in the water. This is called "dolphin jumps". Stand in waist-deep water with knees slightly bent. Bend your torso forward into the water, face down, with your hands and arms in position similar to drill number two. As your arms drive through the stroke, get ready to jump forward as you finish the final scull. Recover your arms over the water in a long dive-glide just as you do in the actual butterfly stroke. Once you are familiar with the action repeat several cycles.

4. The "one-arm fly" is the most popular and useful drill to teach you the rhythmic action of the stroke and the timing of your kicks. Start with your body in the basic glide position and begin kicking. One arm will perform the stroke while the other arm is motionless and extended forward. One kick is performed as your arm begins its stroke. The second kick is performed as your hand passes your navel. Take a breath during the arm recovery and the second kick.

   For this drill, the arm recovery is different than in the regular stroke, because you stretch your arm toward the ceiling to create a slightly sideways kick. The reason for this change in the arm recovery is to allow your body to enter the water with a long glide that brings your hips up and out of the water. Your head, as in the regular stroke, enters the water before your arms do. Your head should dive deeper than normal during entry to create an exaggerated undulation.

   The variations on this drill are limited only by your imagination, or your coach's. For example: change arms every length; swim half a length with one arm, half with the other; do five right and five left, four right and four left, three right and three left, two right and two left, one right and one left, etc.

This drill can also be performed with the resting arm at your side. This variation allows even more undulation because your arm, which was acting as a restrictive forward stabilizer is now removed. However, it is a more advanced drill because it requires greater mechanical control of the stroke. Change arms only at each new length of the pool.

> *Learning tip*
> To help your body undulate, imagine that as your arms and head enter the water, you are crawling under a fence with a sliding action. After the kick and the beginning of the arm action, pretend you are under the fence and your head and shoulders begin to come up on the other side, while you do your second kick and the rest of the arm action.

Breathing

In the butterfly, the breath should be taken late in the stroke, to coincide with the second kick. Late breathing will keep your hips from sinking too soon. The frequency of breathing is up to you. Breathing on every stroke is hard on your legs. Most swimmers breathe on every second arm stroke. But there are as many variations as there are swimmers seriously swimming the fly.

Take a breath, as your hands pass by your stomach, by stretching your neck forward as your shoulders rise. Your face should stay close to the water to avoid forcing your hips down. You should be finished taking the breath by the time the recovering arms are even with your shoulders. Your head can then drop back into the water to allow your arms to do a long reach for the entry. Start breathing out as soon as your head enters the water, so you will be finished in time for the next breath.

> *Points to remember about butterfly breathing*
>
> - Always stretch your neck forward, leading with your chin, to take a breath.
> - Breathe as you complete your second kick. It is better to be late with your breath than early.
> - Take a quick breath, so your head does not stay up longer than necessary.

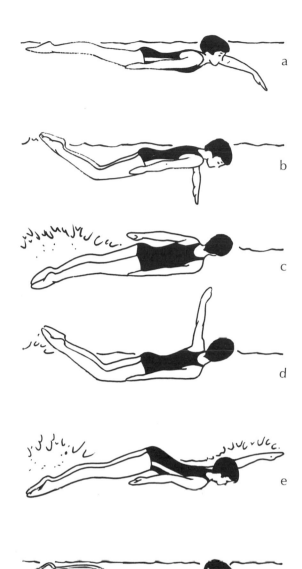

Fig. 4.13. One-arm fly drill with rest arm at side.

Drills

The breathing action and mechanics for the butterfly stroke are similar to the breaststroke, since the head and shoulders work as a unit for both strokes. Use the drills for breaststroke breathing if you need more practice.

Learning progression for the butterfly

Basically the same principles apply as outlined in the other strokes.

1. If you can, watch a film with good butterfly action to show you how it is done and give you some encouragement.

2. Next, establish *correct and strong kicking*, using all the different drills with varying body positions, to help you understand and feel the body undulation. At first, your whole body, including your shoulders, will undulate; later on, kick by limiting the undulation to your hips and legs.

3. Once your kicking technique is strong and confident, you are ready for the *one-arm butterfly*. Be aware of the differences between the one-arm freestyle and the one-arm butterfly, but also recognise the similarities. In the one-arm freestyle, your body rolls with the recovering arms, shoulder first. To control this roll, bend your elbow. In the one-arm fly, swing your arm straight up and around, leading with the hand, to create a long lunging, gliding entry so your hips can come up. Remember that the rest arm is used only as a stabilizer.

4. The *two-arm butterfly* should be practised only after all the previous drills—kicking and arm drills—have been mastered. In training, always use short distances and at first swim the drills without breathing. The distances should be 25, 50 or 75 metres; seldom 100 or 200. The advantage of practising short distances is that you can maintain good form and rhythm at all times. This is the essence of successful butterfly swimming.

The butterfly start

The start in butterfly is similar to the freestyle start. The differences are minor but unique to the stroke. The entry is a little deeper and more curved to propel you into strong kicking. You should attempt to kick four, five, even six times before making the first arm stroke. This is very individual and you will need a lot of training to stay under water for such a long time while performing the kicks in rapid succession. The advantage of staying under water as long as possible is that the drag on your body is

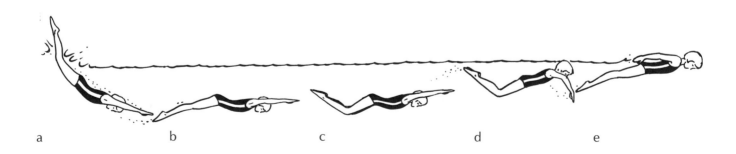

a   b   c   d   e

Fig. 4.14. Butterfly dive-swim out.

less than it is at the surface. When you decide to surface, the last kick should be accompanied by a substantial lift of your head to help the upward and forward slide of your body and begin the arm action. Once you have surfaced you should take at least one stroke before you take the first breath.

Since the butterfly stroke is performed with simultaneous arm and leg actions, there will be a time lapse between the different arm and leg cycles. It is therefore very important to start the stroke powerfully. The objective of the start is to generate immediate power and speed that will help you swim faster.

Learning tip

When your body is submerged, imagine it shaped like a banana. Your body should curve in and then out, as you move into the first stroke.

Points to remember about the butterfly start

- Spring up high when you leave the starting block.
- Allow your back to arch, as you enter the water.
- Make your first kick a strong whip-like action, as you straighten out of the arch.

Drills

Practise the same drills as in freestyle start, but remember to arch your back on entry. Follow through with a strong whip action of the legs.

The butterfly turn

The breaststroke turn and the butterfly stroke turn are identical with only minor body position differences. During the turns, you are governed by the same rules as in the breaststroke. Both hands must touch the wall at the same time and your shoulders must be parallel to the surface when the touch is made. The only difference is that in the fly turn you may take an unlimited number of kicks under water.

In the push-off for the fly, the body position is shallower than in the breaststroke, since the pull-out stroke is different. It is best to take one powerful kick to come near the surface. The second kick and the first arm action will propel you over the surface. As your feet leave the wall, remember to be on your stomach. After a short glide, follow up with a powerful kick.

Learning tip

Keep your shoulders close to the surface of the water as you spin away from the wall.

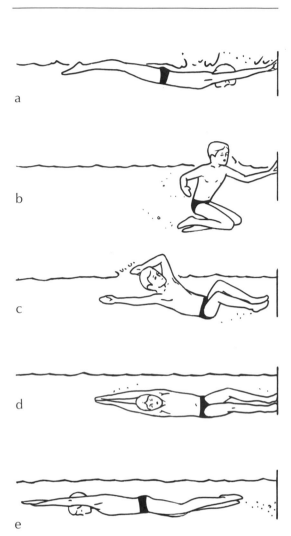

a

b

c

d

e

Fig. 4.15. Butterfly turn.

Points to remember about the butterfly turn

- Plan your approach to the wall from the backstroke turn flags, so that the last recovery will bring your arms to the wall. It is better to be slightly closer to the wall, to keep your body and shoulders high, than to be farther away and possibly approach the turn with your body too low.
- Both hands must touch the wall at the same time and your shoulders must stay horizontal.
- The turn procedure is the same as in the breaststroke.
- Remember that the push-off is shallower than in the breaststroke. But if you are going to try more than one kick, then the push-off should be deep enough to allow this. It is extremely important that your body be fully stretched out, so there will be little drag and your kicking will generate as much speed as possible.
- From the time your feet leave the wall, the procedure should be the same as in the start.

Drills

The approach to the butterfly turn should be the same as the breaststroke, except that the underwater pull-out stroke is not used.

1. Kick to the wall with your arms extended beyond your head. Grab the lip of the pool with both hands — they must touch together. Draw your legs under your body, as you do in the breaststroke. Place your feet on the wall sideways, as your arms leave the wall and your body drops under water about 50 to 60 centimetres. Push out hard and roll onto your front, kicking under water for a chosen number of kicks. Once you can perform the turn well, you should have yourself timed periodically. Check if there is any improvement in the speed of your push-off and the distance you cover.

2. Repeat drill number one, but add a few cycles of the arm stroke without breathing. There are two reasons to hold your breath. You stay more horizontal when your shoulders are not lifted for a breath, and you get immediately the most benefit from your kicking. You will learn also to avoid breathing, at least for the first arm stroke, and focus on assuming the proper body position after the turn instead.

THE INDIVIDUAL MEDLEY

Alex talks about the individual medley

The individual medley is, of course, my favourite event. When I was young, I trained in all four strokes. Being efficient at all four strokes is the goal of the IM swimmer, so for me the IM was a natural progression. I started training IM at 13 and found I was very good at it. The individual medley added variety to my training regime, keeping it from becoming monotonous. That's why I've always loved it.

Strategy is very important in individual medley swimming. It is essential to know your competition. Each swimmer has different strengths and weaknesses in each of the strokes, and the more you know about them the better your chances are of winning the race.

Strategy is especially important in the 400-metre IM because it is such a long, tiring distance — 100 metres of each stroke. The lead may change many times over this distance. Therefore, it is helpful to know how each of your competitors swims the race. You can be easily discouraged by a swimmer who gets an initial lead over you, if you don't know how the swimmer swims the rest of the race. His or her lead may cause you to lose confidence and panic. Keep in mind that it's only the swimmer who leads at the end who wins.

Dr. Tihanyi and I have always believed that the switches between strokes in the IM are of great importance. Each stroke requires the use of different muscle groups, so perfecting switches takes lots of practice. We always worked on trying to accelerate out of each turn. This often gave me a lead because many swimmers have problems adjusting to each of the four strokes.

Individual medley swimmers must work continuously on all four strokes. If one stroke is off, it will affect your times. I believe it is important for young swimmers to train all four strokes and to learn them correctly and efficiently, whether they are aiming for IM competition or not. Correct technique in each stroke is a very important part of becoming a good swimmer. In your later years, you can specialize in the stroke you like best — that is, if you haven't already shown talent in the individual medley.

FACTS ABOUT THE INDIVIDUAL MEDLEY

The individual medley is the performance in combination of the four competitive strokes. Each stroke is performed over one-quarter of the distance, in the following order: butterfly, backstroke, breaststroke and freestyle. The swimming of each stroke and its turn is governed by its respective rules.

The champion individual medley competitor requires lots of experience and training. This is because all four competitive strokes must be perfected for one swimming event. Preparation for the individual medley is the most challenging training of all. The challenge is not only to perfect each style but to combine them into a high level of continuous performance.

Although the individual medley is an exciting competitive event, it has not enjoyed the popularity it deserves. Too many swimming programs focus exclusively on one stroke and don't allow an in-depth exploration of the others. It is, of course, easier to train seriously for a single stroke or event, either sprint or distance. However, if your swim program is based on learning all competitive skills from the very beginning, training for the medley will be an exciting and enjoyable experience that is a natural climax to your training.

In official competition, the individual medley is raced over distances of 200 and 400 metres. But it is perfectly acceptable — and good training — for novice swimmers to compete over 100 metres in local and regional competitions.

The background

Individual medley swimming is the youngest of the swimming disciplines. It has no history that one could connect to ancient times.

Individual medley swimming may have developed from the limitations the four existing strokes created on the sport. Swimmers and their coaches looked for challenges similar to those posed to track and field athletes by the decathlon. By combining the four major competitive strokes, the swimmer was challenged in a new way and the individual medley was created.

The individual medley appeared for the first time at the 1964 Summer Olympic Games.

Objectives for the individual medley

- Swim the combination of the four strokes with confidence and well-executed continuity.
- Distribute your efforts and energy over the entire distance.

The strategy

The allocation of each of the four strokes to one-quarter of the distance does not mean that your effort for each stroke is also equally distributed. No matter how hard you train, you will have strengths and weaknesses in each of the four strokes. Therefore the amount of effort required in the medley will be related to the combination of competition strategy and your ability to perform.

Good athletes develop strategies that will take advantage of their stroke strengths but also allow them to bring out the best in their weak stroke. An intelligently planned race will have athletes gradually increase the effort from the beginning, even if the fly or the backstroke happen to be their strengths. Well-controlled swimming effort at the beginning of the individual medley will keep your body systems in balance, so you can only reach total exhaustion at the very end. This approach to racing requires a lot

The ready position.

MARCO CHIESA

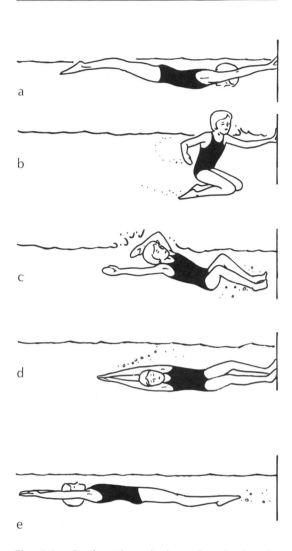

a

b

c

d

e

Fig. 5.1. On-the-side style butterfly-to-backstroke switch.

of confidence in your preparation. Remember that by delaying the onset of fatigue at the beginning, you will be more capable of finishing your race strong and fast.

THE TECHNIQUE

Since the individual medley is the combination of the four strokes already discussed, medley technique relates to the turns or *switches* between the successive strokes. A smooth transition from one style to another without much loss of speed is vital to success in this event.

The turn at the end of a stroke segment is basically the same as has been outlined in the preceding sections. However, each turn requires special attention. Each represents the finish of one stroke and the start of another, and requires immediate adjustment in technique and rhythm. Remember that after each turn your speed will be affected in a different way, because the technical nature of each stroke is different. Each turn will also mean a change in the physical demands you will be making on your body, because each stroke is performed by different muscle actions and the nerves that control them. If anything is difficult about the individual medley, it is this adjustment to the movement pattern of the next style.

Successful individual medley swimmers spend an enormous amount of time perfecting each switch and planning their strategy. It is important to learn to do your turns on both arms (in back-to- breast) and in both directions (in butterfly-to-back and breast-to-freestyle), so that you have more options when you plan your swim strategy.

Individual medley switch turns

The butterfly-to-backstroke switch
There are two popular options for leaving the wall at the end of this turn. Both are simple, but one may suit you or your situation better than the other. The approach to the wall is the same as in the regular fly turn. But as your hands are about to touch the wall together, your legs should begin to bend at the knees. Draw them up to your chest and, at the same time, drop your head between your arms. This is done so you can quickly place your feet on the wall and do a very powerful push- off that will maintain your speed and help you adjust to the backstroke.

Option A: Immediately after the touch, as your feet are swinging under water toward the wall, push one hand away and stretch it alongside and over your head, rotating your body slightly to the side of the outstretched arm. This move will position your body stretched along its side, for the coming push-off. The feet are placed on the wall with the toes pointing diagonally up. Push off hard with the other hand and both legs. Then, reach your pushing hand along your head to quickly join your outstretched arm.

Option B: Use the same approach as in Option A, but keep both hands on the wall while your legs come up and under your body. Like a pendulum, swing your body forward under water, so your feet are placed on the wall while your hands push off. Your shoulders will fall back as you reach your arms above your head, while your legs push off hard in a streamlined stretch through the water.

In Option A, you leave the wall slightly on your side and roll completely onto your back as you begin kicking. In Option B, you leave the wall on your back. From this point on, the procedure is exactly the same as the push-off in the regular backstroke turn. The depth of the push-off should be about 30 centimetres or one body depth to allow you to surface quickly. The only difference from the regular backstroke push-off is that in the individual medley it is important to start stroking and breathing without delay, in order to quickly complete your adjustment to the next style.

> *Learning tip*
> The approach to the wall must always be fast and carefully planned.

> *Learning tip*
> The time you spend on the wall, from hand touch to the time your feet push off, should not exceed one second.

The backstroke-to-breaststroke switch

Again there are two ways to make this switch. Both of these should be learned in case unforeseen conditions make one of the options unsuitable.

The approach to the wall is similar to the regular backstroke approach. Keep up your strong kicking and count in from the turn flag. Be sure to stay on your back until you touch the wall.

Option A: This is the back somersault-to-breaststroke switch. On the last arm stroke to the wall, your head and shoulders will follow the leading arm under water. Put your hand on the wall at a depth of about 50 to 60 centimetres to force your hips and legs to come to the surface. At that point, your bent knees will be lifted out over the water and move to a slight tuck toward your chest. Simultaneously, the hand on the wall should push away hard, throwing your head back further in the somersault spin action that will put you onto your stomach. Your feet will land on the wall at approximately the same spot where your hand was. As soon as they are firmly on the wall, push hard to drive your body away from the

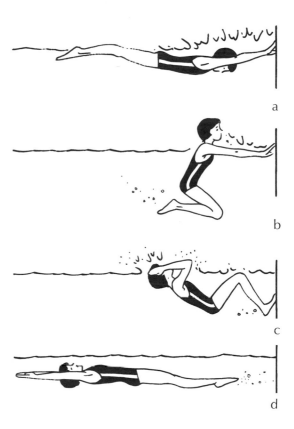

Fig. 5.2. Pendulum style butterfly-to-backstroke switch.

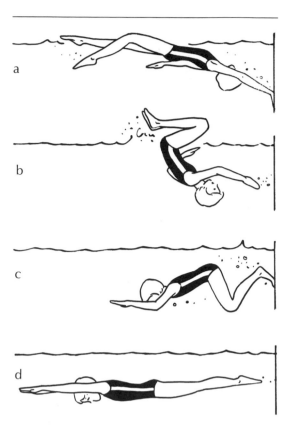

Fig. 5.3.   Somersault style backstroke-to-breaststroke switch.

wall. From this point on, the procedure is the same as in the breaststroke underwater pull-out.

Option B: This is the open-bucket backstroke-to-breaststroke switch. The last arm stroke to the wall is the same as in the ordinary bucket turn. As your feet come out of the water, your hand will push hard off the wall and start your body spin. Lift your head for a breath and drop your knees to allow your feet to head for the wall. It is important that your body rotate quickly onto its side, so your feet can also rotate to land on the wall sideways. Your arms are swung up along your head, lining up for the drive off the wall into a long stretch. At this point, you may be on your side. But it is better to be closer to being on your chest than on your back as your feet leave the wall. From this point on, continue the breaststroke underwater pull-out.

It is worth noting that there is no advantage to staying under water over a long distance during the underwater pull-out, even though a breath is taken during the turn. Swimming the 400-metre individual medley is very demanding and a continuous supply of oxygen is more important than prolonging the glide to minimize drag.

Learning tip
Always drive yourself away from the wall with the hardest push you can manage.

The breaststroke-to-freestyle switch
This is the simplest and probably fastest switch of the three. In this case, you have only one choice in making the turn. The approach is the same as in the regular breaststroke turn and the same rules apply for the touch and body position. The spin away from the wall is also the same as in the breaststroke turn. The only difference is the speed at which your hands push away from the wall. Once you have touched the wall, there are no specific rules for the rest of the turn. So you can freely and speedily move off the wall as fast as you can manage.

Move one hand away first to help your body to twist onto its side for a quick push-off. After you have stretched the first arm away from the wall over your head, your feet are being planted on the wall sideways. Now your second arm joins the first. Drive yourself away from the wall stretched out on your side.

This push-off should be shallow with little time spent under water. Start kicking immediately and then take your first arm stroke. The adjustment from the breaststroke to freestyle is very difficult and the sooner you start kicking and stroking, the easier it will be.

Learning tip
Once you have mastered the basics, always practise switching at top speed to help the physical adaptation from one stroke to the next. For this reason, the practice distance should be short.

Things to remember about the individual medley

- Learn to increase your effort gradually as you progress through the four strokes.
- Always kick hard in approaching your switches.
- A quick switch will get you off the wall fast, so you can carry your approach speed to the next stroke.

Drills
You have already learned and practised the mechanics of each of the four styles and their respective turns. Try the individual medley only after you have learned the basics of each stroke and turn. The only new skill in medley turns will be to learn to switch efficiently from one stroke to the next.

1. First "walk" through each switch in waist-deep water, so the adjustment to the next style can be made slowly and consciously. That is, perform the approach by going through the motion of each arm action, turn and switch slowly and deliberately and swim away from the wall, using the individual medley stroke order.

2. Swim to the wall with a few strokes in the fly, turn and switch to the backstroke. Kick away from the wall powerfully without using your arms. Repeat this for each switch. Using only your legs will help you concentrate on the correct body position as you leave the wall, increase your awareness of the importance of strong kicking as you start the next stroke and get the large muscles in your body used to the process of switching.

3. Add the appropriate arm action once you are confident in the switching process. Again, swim a short distance into and away from the wall and concentrate on the switching technique and the power of the drive off the wall. Ten- to 15-metre swims in and out are enough to get some speed for a quick switch. The order of the repeat swims are: fly-back, back-breast, breast-free.

4. At the next level, practise 25-metre approach distances. "Switching" drills should not be practised over distances longer than 25 metres.

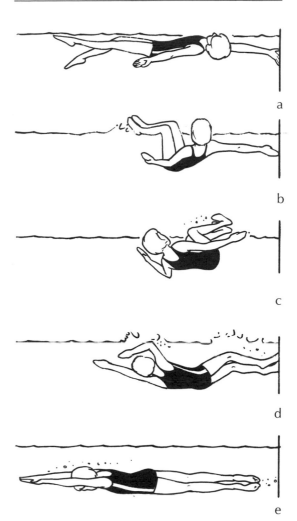

Fig. 5.4. Open-bucket style backstroke-to-breast stroke switch.

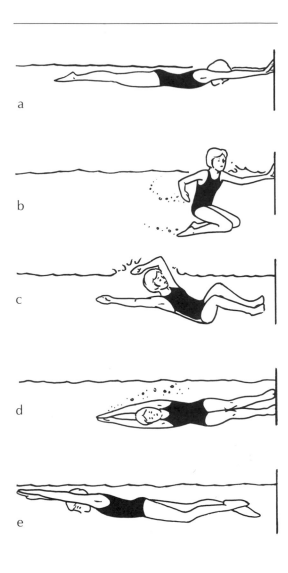

Fig. 5.5.   Breaststroke-to-freestyle switch.

The finishing touch

Electronic timing for races—whether they are specific stroke competitions or individual medleys—has taken over the more traditionally timed visual judgements of the past. Electronic timing in competitive swimming demands a more aggressive and better planned approach to the finish of a race on the part of the swimmer. With electronic timing, the first person to touch the timing pad is the winner. Electronic timing judges to the thousandth of a second and rounds to the hundredth of a second. Winners are often declared by a difference of only one one-hundredth of a second. Such close races are virtually impossible to time visually.

This fine judgement demands special skills for the finishing swimmer. It is, therefore, very important to be sensitive to the demands of the finish and develop your finishing skills well. The more you practise these skills, the easier you will find them. Eventually the finish approach will become an automatic element in your race repertoire. Luckily the approaches to the turns are similar, therefore these skills can complement both your turns and finishes.

The sequence of skills is as follows: increase the rate of your kicking gradually, starting about 15 metres away from the finish wall. For butterfly and breaststroke, because both legs kick at the same time, you should start increasing your kicking farther away, at about 25 metres. The point of harder kicking is not only to help you with the speed, but also to elevate your body so your arms can stroke more easily. Begin to control the frequency of your breathing so your body is even more streamlined, and the increased kicking will be even more effective. Fix your eyes on the end wall target (turning cross), as you are getting closer to the wall for a better forward stretch of your body and a higher body position. Adjust your stroke (shorten or lengthen) as you are swimming by the five-metre mark to ensure an exact touch. From here until the finish, no breath should be taken. Kick furiously. For the last forward reach of your arm, stretch your shoulder forward and keep your head at the shoulder level to shave off those last fractions of a second.

A recent photograph: I still train three times a week.

MARCO CHIESA

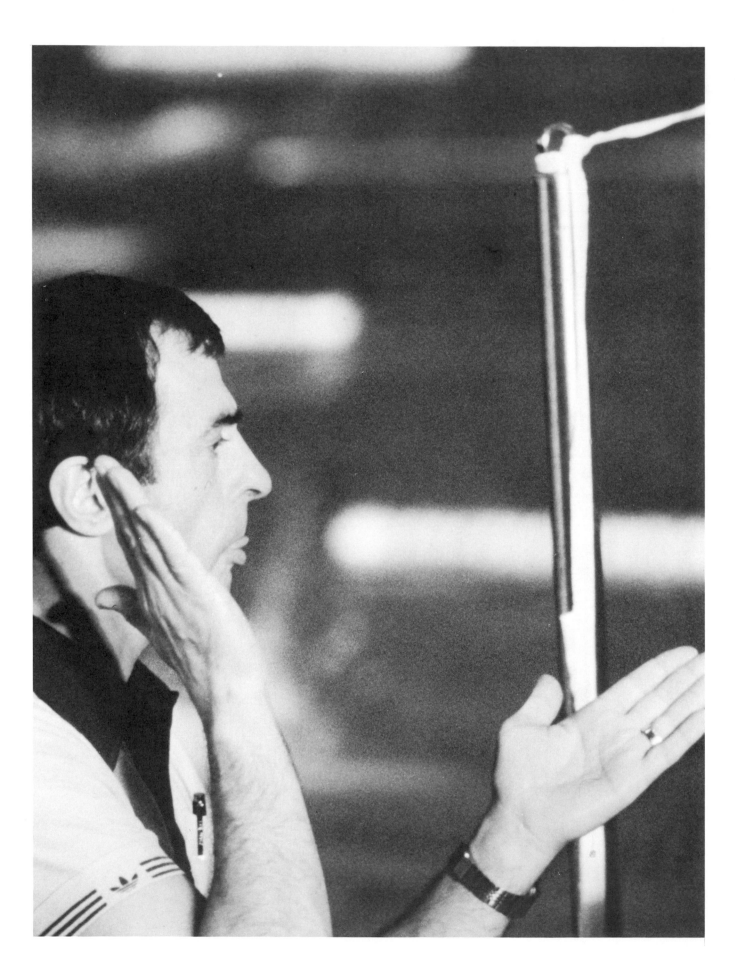

TRAINING FOR THE COMPETITIVE SWIMMER

When you see your favourite athletes winning world championships and Olympic medals, do you wonder how they became as good as they are? Is it their natural talent that has given them the edge over others? Chances are, if you could look back over the swimming careers of these athletes, you would find that they started out very much as you did, and that they, too, had swimming heroes and wondered what the secret to *their* success was. Natural ability is not all it takes and skills are learned and developed rather than inherited. The secret of these successful athletes lies in hard work and *training*.

Training is the physical preparation of your body over a long period of time—often many years—to perform the strokes to the very best of your ability. Your ability, called your *potential*, is unknown to you when you begin training. Your skill level is only at the beginning stages. With frequent training, you will notice how quickly you can make progress in your skills and in your ability to swim for longer distances without stop. With good training habits, and proper guidance from your coach if you have one, you will realize your potential. But be prepared to work at it for several years. No one can become a skilled swimmer overnight.

Always begin with small goals and work your way up. Your first goals should be to develop good stroke skills and to increase your endurance. This is the focus of *novice training*. In the section on novice training, you will find tips for those who are just beginning their swim careers. As you advance, your goals and the focus of your training will change. The section on *advanced training* gives advice for those who have been swimming for several years. Whether you are a novice or an advanced swimmer, you can benefit from reading both sections.

Not all training is done in the water. In fact, most training begins on land. The section on *land training* describes exercises that all swimmers in training should do to build up strength and endurance.

In addition to training the body, it is important to train the mind. Your body is not merely a machine that will function if you give it the right exercise. What you think about your training has an effect on the way you perform. Your mind has to be willing and dedicated. In the section on *training your mind*, you will learn the importance of having a positive attitude and being committed to achieving your goals.

It is very difficult to train alone. Like most things in life, it is much easier to achieve your goals when there are others to guide you, support you and even share your goals. This is why most

Dr. Jeno Tihanyi on the pool deck at the Olympic Trials in Toronto in 1984.

ATHLETE INFORMATION BUREAU

swimmers prefer *training with a swim team*. On a swim team, you will have a coach to guide and instruct you and teammates to share in both your larger and smaller goals. Your coach and your teammates are there to support you, just as you are there to support your teammates. Together, you can encourage one another to train hard and strive to do better and better.

A good training program must be based on knowledge about the body and how it works. The more you understand about the systems of your body and how they relate to your training—how your heart rate affects your swimming, why you need more oxygen to swim well—the more effective your training will be. The section on *swimming and your body* discusses what you can do to help the systems of your body work together efficiently, so that you can train to the best of your potential.

It is equally important to know how the food you eat affects your body and gives you the energy you need to swim and train hard. The section on *swimming and nutrition* outlines the basic nutrition you need and gives sample menu plans you can follow.

Swimming is not like hockey for which you need a large bag to hold lots of heavy equipment. When you think of swimming, you probably think only of a swimsuit, cap and goggles. But as you make progress in your training, you need more equipment to train effectively. The section on *equipment and training aids* describes the basic equipment you will need.

The purpose of training is to realize your potential. You may not even know what your potential is when you begin. You may surprise yourself, your coach and your parents by swimming better than any of you realized you could. The most important thing to learn about training is that you must be prepared to work hard. Of course, as you get better at swimming, training will be fun too, especially when you are able to swim better and faster with less effort. Through a well-planned program and your determination to follow it, you, too, might one day become someone's swimming hero.

TRAINING THE NOVICE SWIMMER

You don't have to be young to be a novice swimmer. A novice is merely someone who has just begun to train. In novice training, you concentrate on learning good stroke skills.

Most novice swimmers, however, are between the ages of six to 13 years of age. At this age, your body is still changing, which means that the way you do your strokes is still changing. Therefore, even if you have been training for several years, you are still not ready for advanced training. Until your body stops growing and changing, it is better to concentrate on learning your skills and doing your strokes well. This is what novice training does.

As a novice, the most important thing you need to remember is not how fast you swim, but how *well* you perform your strokes. In addition to learning good technique, you should concentrate on increasing your *endurance capacity*. Endurance is the ability of your body to continue an activity for a prolonged period of time. Your endurance capacity develops slowly over many years of training. As you train and as your body grows, so will your endurance capacity increase.

Some words from Alex

When I first joined the club as a novice swimmer, I trained three times a week and regarded swimming as more of a social event than a competitive sport. By the time I was 10, I had gradually increased my training to seven times a week. Although it worked for me, I would not recommend such a difficult schedule for every beginning swimmer.

Training hard to develop good stroke skills is important for the novice swimmer, but too much pressure at the beginning can cause a young swimmer to quit, or burn out early. I believe that there should be time put aside during training for having fun in the water. Water polo and relay races, for example, will keep young swimmers happy and interested.

Skill development tips

As you begin any skill training, you must learn to listen to instructions and to co-operate in a group. You must also learn how to use your training equipment and how to take care of it.

Develop your kicking skills first. It is important that you learn the correct kick patterns for the different strokes, so that you can perform them automatically, without thinking about them. This will make it easier for you to practise the arm drills and to do the whole stroke.

You cannot practise kicking too often. The more you do it, the more automatic it will become. Practise all the drills outlined in each stroke section with and without the kickboard.

Spend equal amounts of time on each of the four strokes. As you get older and become more advanced, it will become clear which stroke(s) you are best in. Then is the time for specialization. You may find that you like all the strokes and are suited for the individual medley.

One way you can build up good stroke skills and endurance is through continuous or *sustained swimming*. This is swimming that is done slowly for a certain length of time, rather than for a certain distance at high speed.

The best way to perfect strokes is through *drill swimming*. In drill swimming, you concentrate on only one part of your stroke at a time. For instance, you do several lengths of right arm only, then several lengths of left arm only. Or you focus on the recovery, the entry, or how your hand is held, and so on. At first, drill swimming should always be done slowly, so that you can concentrate on doing each stroke as accurately as possible. It is easier for your coach or instructor to correct your strokes when you are going slowly. As you perfect your skills, add some speed to your drills.

As you become better at the strokes, you can combine drill swimming with continuous and *whole stroke swimming*. In whole stroke swimming, you concentrate on the feel of the whole stroke, rather than just one part as in drill swimming, although your coach may ask you to think of one part only. In combining drill and whole stroke swimming, you could, for example, swim right arm only for six strokes, left arm only for six strokes, and six strokes with both arms. Do this routine for several minutes.

Some words from Alex

As novice swimmers at Laurentian University Swim Club, we often watched swimming films or tapes to improve our skills. This was very helpful because we could then copy what the people in the films were doing. When you watch the stroke being performed correctly, it is much easier to see your own mistakes.

Endurance development tips

Develop your kicking endurance first by doing the kicking drills for long periods of time. This type of kicking is done at a slower pace, so you can be sure you're doing it correctly. The distance you cover is not as important at first as being able to go continuously for a period of time without stopping. Increase your kicking time by 15 seconds or more each week in each stroke, to gradually gain endurance. The total time you spend kicking should be done both with and without the kickboard.

Once you are able to do each style of kicking for a reasonable length of time, practise kicking in the individual medley order. When you change from one type of kicking to the next, increase the time you spend on it. For example, if you do the butterfly kick for two minutes, next do the backstroke kick for two minutes and thirty seconds, and so on. This way you will simulate the stress that you may experience in the individual medley.

At the same time as you are increasing your kicking endurance, increase the time you spend swimming in each session. If you have a coach, you can plan a program of increased time for up to a year in advance, with different time goals for each month. For example, start with short time intervals of one minute swimming and 30 seconds resting. Use the rest period to go over a particular part of your stroke that needs work. If you are practising freestyle, focus on not breathing for three arm movements before and after the turns for one time interval. For the next time interval, focus on kicking hard toward and away from the wall for about five metres at each turn, and so on.

Increase the length of the swim periods by 15 to 30 seconds, at first by the week, then later according to a plan you and your coach develop. It is important that you don't stop during these swim periods, so that you will get an accurate idea of how well you are building up your endurance. But, at the same time, don't push yourself too hard. If you find your stroke beginning to deteriorate, you probably need to take a rest.

Do not rest for too long between swim periods, or you will recover too well and perform the next swim too quickly. Short rests will build up your endurance more effectively. Gradually you will find you need fewer rest periods.

Begin by practising each stroke separately. When you can do the strokes in the time that you and your coach have set as your goal (sustained swimming for, say, 20 minutes), you can then begin to do the strokes together in the individual medley pattern for the 20 minutes. For instance, change strokes every 15 seconds on the sound of a whistle until the 20 minutes are up.

Although your focus is *not* on speed at this time, you will find that, as your endurance increases, your speed will increase naturally. In order to figure out how your speed is increasing, count the number of lengths you do in a given period of time. Record the number each time you swim. You will probably find you are able to do more and more lengths as time goes on.

Learning to count the number of lengths you do is important, because you will have to keep track in a distance event such as the 400-, 800- or 1500-metre freestyle. Remember, again, that speed is not as important right now as technique and endurance.

Learn to glance at the pace clock while swimming, so that you can see how long it takes you to do each length and so you learn to keep the same time for each length. In this way, you will develop an even pace.

As the final part of your endurance development, begin to swim the specific competitive distances. For example, do each stroke for the 200-metre, the freestyle for the 400-, 800- and 1500-metre, and the individual medley for the 200- and 400-metre. Arrange for someone to time your distances. You are now ready to begin concentrating on improving your times.

How often should novice swimmers train?
How often you should train depends on how old you are and how well you perform your strokes. Swimmers under the age of 10 shouldn't train more than three times a week for an hour at a time. Those who are older than 10 should begin with three sessions a week as well, but this can be increased to four sessions (again no more than one hour per session). Keep to these limits for the first two or three years. After this, you can increase the

number of sessions to five or even six. This will depend on your own ability and endurance. Remember to increase the number of sessions gradually.

Some words from Alex

Endurance training should be practised early in a swimmer's career. In later years, when specialization occurs, you won't need as much endurance work, because your body will be more accustomed to swimming long and hard.

I worked on developing endurance by working out and doing exercises which maintained my heart rate for extended periods of time. I also practised sets with ascending effort. This builds endurance because, even when you are getting tired, you must still swim faster and try harder.

Points to remember about novice training

- Remember, how *well* you do your strokes is more important than how *fast* you do them.
- Develop your stroke technique first, and then build up your endurance by increasing the number and length of swim sets.
- Do not rest for too long between each swim repeat. If you swim for one minute, rest for thirty seconds.
- Once you have built up your endurance, you can begin to think about increasing your speed.

TRAINING THE ADVANCED SWIMMER

After you have learned all the fundamental skills, have acquired good technique in each stroke and have developed your endurance, you are ready for advanced training. To learn all the skills for every stroke may take you six years. The younger you are when you start organized swimming, the longer it takes to grow out of the novice rank. You must wait until your body has done most of its growing. The body needs extra energy during adolescence, when it is going through a great number of physical changes. After you reach your growth peak, then your body will be able to put energy into more serious training. For girls this will usually be by age 12 or 13, and for boys by age 15 or sometimes 16.

Advanced swimming is the time to begin concentrating on the specific strokes at which you are best. It should now be clear what your strengths and weaknesses are. This is the time to decide whether you should specialize in one stroke or continue development in the individual medley. You will also soon know whether you are best at sprints, middle distances or long distances.

There are two training and competitive distances in the year-long advanced training program: the short course (for competitions in a 25-metre pool) and the long course (for competitions in a 50-metre pool). The competitive year is usually 11 months long. The short course, therefore, lasts for five months, and the long course for six months.

In both courses, the training program is usually divided into four time periods. These are: (1) the early season or pre-competitive period; (2) the mid-season or competitive period; (3) the final preparatory period; and (4) the taper or peaking period. The length of each period depends on when the championship swim meet may be, that is, how long the short course or the long course season may be. Usually, the early season takes about four to six weeks, the mid-season eight weeks and the final preparatory and peaking period about six weeks. In each of these periods, you will concentrate on a particular part of your training to prepare you for the competition.

Some words from Alex
*As an advanced swimmer, I trained about five hours a day —
three-and-a-half hours of swimming and one-and-a-half hours of
land training. In three-and-a-half hours of swimming, I would
sometimes cover up to 16 kilometres. Sometimes this was very
monotonous, but we held competitions to break it up.*

The early season or pre-competitive period
Since this is the first period of the new season, when you probably haven't had any training for several weeks, this is the time to get your body back into condition. It is also the time to learn new

rules and new goals for the season and to learn to work with your new teammates.

Out of the pool, you will probably do some cross-country running to increase your general fitness level and calisthenics to loosen up the muscles and joints. (See the section on "Land Training".) After about two to three weeks, you should begin weight training. But make sure that your training involves the whole body. It is important to do stretching and flexibility exercises along with the weight training.

In the pool, you will begin with slow and continuous swimming to gradually build up your stamina and to ensure that you re-establish a good technique. Even if you are going to specialize in sprints, you still need to build up stamina. You should do occasional sprint sets to begin to prepare your body for speed.

Concentrate on developing good starting and turning techniques early in the season. As the season progresses, you will eventually perform over 400 turns daily, so it is very important that you learn proper technique at the beginning of the season.

Your training should begin slowly and be aimed at endurance development at about 60 to 70 per cent of your ability, based on your previous year's best times. Similarly, your heart rate should be matched to your swimming effort. The heart rate that you generate with a certain swimming effort corresponds closely, but not exactly, to that effort. For example, if you are swimming at 70 per cent of your best time, your heart rate should also be at 70 per cent of its maximum exercise ability. To find your heart's maximum exercise ability is simple. *Maximum exercise heart rate* (MEHR) equals 220 minus your age. For example if you are 16 years of age, then your MEHR equals 204 (220 minus 16). So 70 per cent of 204 is the appropriate heart rate for your 70 per cent effort swim. In this example, then, your swimming heart rate should be 143 beats per minute (70 per cent of 204 equals 143). By frequently taking your heart rate, you should be able to control your speed. The slower your speed, the slower your heart beats and, of course, the faster you swim the faster your heart beats. Slow heart rate swimming is appropriate for endurance development, so you should keep your heart rate during this training season mostly below 160. As your fitness level improves, you can occasionally increase your swimming speed to perhaps 80 per cent of maximum ability. If, for example, your last year's time for the 400-metre freestyle was five minutes, you should aim to repeat this distance in training in six minutes. Add 20 per cent to your last year's best, to get the 80 per cent time.

When you swim a certain percentage of your best time, you always add time to your training time because your best time is 100 per cent. If you swim something at 80 per cent then you go 20 per cent slower, therefore you add 20 per cent to your best time. As you increase the percentage of your training times, you also increase the response of your heart to the faster swims. This means your heart rate per minute will be higher. It is a good idea to learn how fast your heart beats per minute for the different percentage of training repeats you practise.

The number of sessions at the beginning of the season should be no more than five per week, preferably in the afternoon. This number should be increased gradually so that by the end of the pre-competitive period the total number of sessions will be eight per week, with three mornings and five afternoons, totalling about 14 hours.

The mid-season or competitive period

During the mid-season or competitive period, you will practise your improved technique under the stress of actual competition and begin to develop new strategies. It is important to participate in competitions frequently during this time.

You will now begin to concentrate on the stroke(s) and distance(s) you want to specialize in, and you and your teammates will begin to follow different programs best suited to the needs of your individual specialties. These programs may vary in length and number of training sessions.

The number of training sessions may be increased to a maximum of 11. The usual pattern is six mornings and five evenings, totalling approximately 21 to 23 hours of water training.

Race pace swimming (swimming at the speed you would hope to swim during the actual competition) is introduced with *descending swimming* and *broken swimming*. In descending swim sets, your objective is to go faster for each successive repeat in the set. With this type of training, you are attempting to simulate the way your body should feel in an actual race. You are trying to go faster and faster, in spite of the gradually increasing fatigue of your body.

In broken swim sets, you divide the race distance in portions like quarters or thirds or halves with a five- to 15-second rest between each segment. This way you will be able to swim faster than during the actual race where you have no rest periods. This type of swim sets teaches you how to judge your pace without being too careful and swimming below your ability.

It is essential that long sets of repeats are practised with specific pace requirements that will help you to learn to judge the effort required to maintain a specific speed. It is also essential to occasionally swim faster than race speed over shorter distances to help your body get used to putting out maximum effort.

Toward the end of the competitive period, you should begin to train at the specific distance at which you're going to compete. You should now be putting out at over 85 per cent of your ability.

Be careful not to become exhausted from over-training. It is important that you alternate between hard and easy days so your body can recover. Compete frequently, not only to measure your progress, but also so that your body will become used to the stress of competition. Low level competitions are also a good opportunity to practise strategies.

Don't forget your kicking skills. Every training session should include some endurance kicking and some sprint kicking.

In this period, land training should include specific weight training to increase your strength for your specific races. Remember that along with weight training, daily stretching is a must. Stretching should be done before and after each session.

Some words from Alex

I learned the basic strategies needed to perform my best in competition during the competitive period. Things such as descending sets and broken sets in training helped me get the most out of myself. At this point, I was training 11 times a week. I found that when I disciplined myself to go to every workout, it became a routine, just like brushing my teeth.

The final preparatory period

This period represents the last four weeks of actual preparation before the taper period and the final major swim meet. During this time, you will concentrate exclusively on the event you are going to compete in, and fine-tune your stroke and strategy.

Reduce the number of training sessions during this period of intense training by cutting out some of the morning sessions. You will be putting out at almost your maximum ability and will need to make sure you have enough recovery time between sessions. Eight sessions at the beginning of this period is probably satisfactory, and this number should be reduced to five by the end.

Broken swims, dive swims and all-out sprints should dominate the day-to-day training routine. Dive swims are important, since you need to practise your dive and your ability to sprint out of dive starts. You can easily combine dive swims with broken swims and all-out sprints. All-out sprints should be over the 25- and 50-metre distances. If you want to go longer than 50 metres in your all-out swims, then combine them with broken swims. And don't forget to give sufficient time to kicking.

Reduce your land training to about two sessions per week. At this time, it should be gradually directed to speed work. In the weight room, the weight exercises should be light but fast with repetitions of up to 50 to 60 for each routine.

Stretching, of course, should be continued daily to keep your muscles loose and to help the recovery process.

You should participate in at least one competition at about the third week of this period, to see if you need to work on anything in addition to fine-tuning.

Some words from Alex

The final preparatory period and the taper period are very important and probably the hardest time in a swimmer's program. You have to train hard, but you also have to be rested for the big race. You must stay mentally and physically focused and perform to the limits of your potential at every workout.

We prepared for an important race, at least one month in advance, by cutting down on total distances and putting more emphasis on starts, turns and sprinting. I started resting more and more as the competition drew nearer, and I stayed focused on the times I wanted to achieve.

Points to remember about training the advanced swimmer

- Begin and end every training session with stretches to loosen your muscles and prevent injuries.
- At the beginning of the season, make sure you re-establish good technique in strokes and turns before you concentrate on improving times.
- Participate at first in low-level competitions before you enter important ones. You need to get used to the stress of competition and to practise strategies. Later you can attempt to improve times.
- Resting is an important part of demanding training. Without adequate rest between swimming sessions, your body will not function at its best.

The taper or peaking period

You enter into the taper or peaking period when you are just about 14 days away from the major competition. These final days should be spent on fine-tuning, both physically and mentally.

Resting is an important part of this period. If you are a sprinter, reduce your training sessions to four and then three per week. If you are a distance swimmer, keep the number of sessions at five or more. The intensity of distance training is less, therefore shorter recovery is required.

Part of every training session should be spent on low level aerobic work to keep up your endurance and help your recovery rate. This type of swimming keeps your heart rate low and does not accumulate any waste products in your muscles. It also allows you to recheck your skills after many weeks of intense training.

Drop all land training except light stretching before and after sessions in the pool.

Sprinters should practise-dive 25-metre sprints and establish the final strategy. Distance swimmers should maintain pace work but reduce the number of repetitions and allow sufficient recovery time.

Refine your turns with short sprint in-and-out drills. Sprint to the end wall from about 10 metres out, so you can generate adequate speed. Turn and sprint out about 10 metres with strong kicking and preferably holding your breath.

Don't forget to save time for fun and relaxation!

Time out: it's as necessary to enjoy your time in the water as it is to train hard.

MARCO CHIESA

LAND TRAINING

Land training is as important as swimming training, no matter how old or how advanced you are. There are so many different kinds of exercises with different levels of difficulty that there will always be something to challenge you, whether you are a beginner or a world champion.

If you are a beginner or novice swimmer, you should spend about half of your total training time on the various kinds of land training exercises. If you are an advanced swimmer, you should spend a quarter to a third of all training on land. This does not mean land training becomes less important as you advance. It means that the novice swimmer has a great deal more to learn and has a longer way to go to build up strength.

The most popular land training programs include stretching, calisthenics, tumbling and agility activities, running and weight training. Each activity has a place and time in the yearly program.

Some words from Alex

Land training is very important for increasing strength and providing some variation from swimming. I run, lift weights, climb ropes, run stairs and do swim bench. All these exercises help my performance in the pool.

Dr. Tihanyi devised a regime of land training that was the right balance between strength and endurance. Often I climbed ropes or performed jumping jacks to increase both arm and leg strength. I ran at the beginning of each season to get into cardiovascular shape, and did weight training to build strength.

Stretching

Before you do any other exercises on land or in the water, you must do stretching exercises. Stretching the muscles and the tissue around your joints will prevent injuries. Stretching *after* a workout will increase your blood supply, so that your muscles will not need as much time to recover. Most swimmers develop a routine that stretches every part of their body.

Stretching increases your overall flexibility. As a swimmer, you need to be as flexible as possible to perform your strokes to the best of your ability. You cannot swim very well or very fast if you are stiff and sore.

Younger swimmers are often naturally flexible and able to put their bodies into all kinds of extraordinary positions. They may think they don't need to do warm-up stretches. But remember, the older they become, the less flexible they are. All swimmers, whatever their age, should do stretching exercises before and after every training session—on land and in the water—both to keep their flexibility and to increase it.

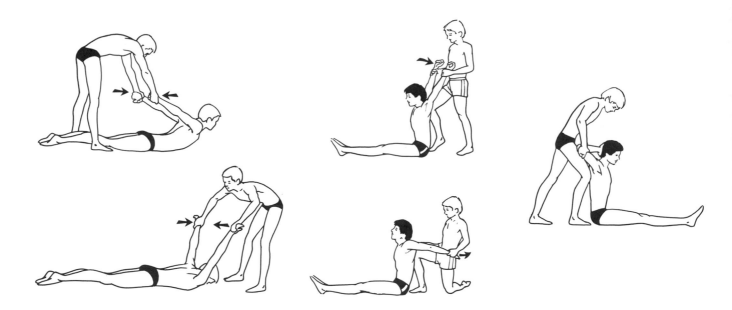

Partner-assisted shoulder stretching exercises. The pull should be slow, and held at the extreme position for 10–20 seconds.

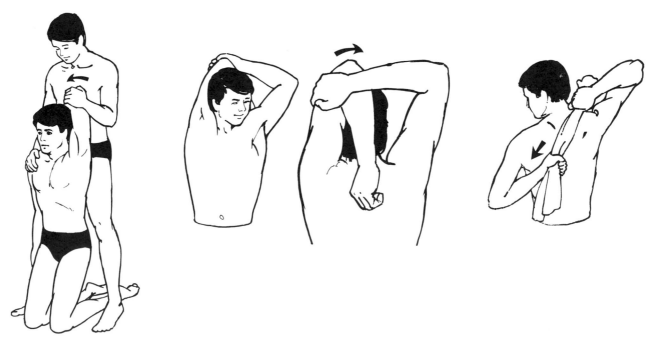

Partner-assisted and unassisted single shoulder stretching exercises. Hold stretched position for 10–30 seconds.

The accompanying illustrations show just some examples of stretching exercises. You may pick up others by watching other swimmers perform their routines.

Some words from Alex

Stretching exercises prevent injuries such as muscle pulls and tears or tendonitis. These exercises help to stretch out the muscles and tendons before a workout. A workout puts a lot of stress on muscles and tendons. If they've been properly stretched out with exercises, their elasticity and ability to withstand the lengthening and shortening of muscles during the workout is increased.

Calisthenics

Along with stretches, calisthenics are used as the first step in the general warm-up procedure, which is often referred to as limbering up. These exercises include head rotations, neck stretches, arm circles, trunk rotations, twists and bends, leg and ankle circles, and some hops. These kinds of exercises will increase your flexibility, loosen up muscles to avoid injuries, and make your movements in the water more graceful.

Doing calisthenics will also tone your muscles and may even increase your body strength, so that even when you get tired you will be able to maintain your body position in the water. Usually when you get tired, your body position begins to deteriorate and your strokes deteriorate. This process is similar to what happens when the bottom of a boat has a hole in it: it flounders a little before it sinks. Strengthening your abdominal and lower back muscles will prevent you from "sinking". The best exercises for strengthening the abdominal and lower back muscles are sit ups and back extension or back bends.

Tumbling and agility activities

These exercises are useful if you are a novice swimmer. They will help you discover the many different ways you can move your body. Then, when you are in the water and are learning skills like the freestyle turn, you will know how that movement will *feel*, because you've done forward rolls on land. Novice swimmers should do these activities all year before every water training session for about 20 to 30 minutes.

Running

Because swimming is mostly an indoor activity, an outdoor activity such as running may be a welcome change. You can run outside through September, October and November, weather permitting. Cross-country running with the team can be an exciting experience in wooded areas, up and down hills, perhaps ending with a game of soccer.

Running will improve your cardiovascular system (heart, lungs,

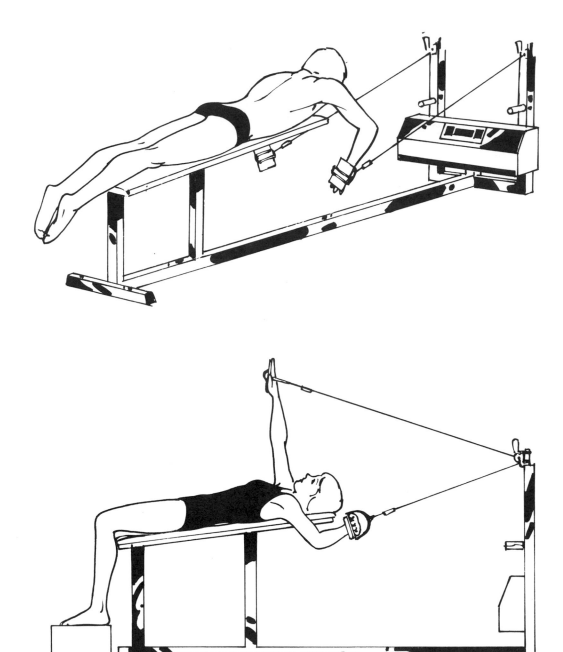

The biokinetic swim bench: to be effective, exercises must closely imitate the actual path of the stroke in the water. In (a) swimmer practises butterfly arm action, and in (b) backstroke.

circulation). Initially you should combine running with walking, and then, as you become more fit, you can decrease the amount of walking. For example, run five minutes and walk one minute for a few days, then run ten minutes and walk one minute, and so on.

Be careful when running on rough or bumpy ground so that you don't injure your ankles and knees. Don't spend more than 30 minutes on running activities, and always do warm-up and cool-down stretches.

After two to three weeks of cross-country running, you will be ready to do some stair running or steep-hill running. If your swimming pool building does not have longer staircases and if you cannot find a conveniently located building for stair running, perhaps you may find a hill nearby and do your running there. At first, walk up and run down to avoid injuries. If you combine stair running with cross-country running, do it for no more than 40 minutes.

Once you can run uphill or upstairs with ease, you can begin to increase your speed, making sure you have adequate rest intervals. This exercise will condition the legs for pushing off the wall, for diving off the block and for some kicking movements. You can do stair running all through the year indoors, until you reach the final preparatory phase and the taper period if you are an advanced swimmer.

Weight training

Weight training is very important for all swimmers. It will increase your overall strength and lower your chances of injury. The particular kind of weight training you do will depend on whether you are a novice or an advanced swimmer. Novice swimmers should concentrate on increasing overall strength. Advanced swimmers should concentrate on the particular muscle groups they use in the stroke(s) they specialize in and on the distances they swim.

Always warm up using the stretching and calisthenic exercises outlined above to avoid injuries. And always stretch out well after each session.

During your first few sessions, make sure you have the correct technique. Then slowly increase the weight you lift or the number of repetitions you do.

Early in the season, determine your *optimal training weight* (OTW). Estimate this by finding the weight that you can move in an exercise eight times to nearly failure (that is, you are almost unable to complete the eighth lift). Determine your pure strength specific or endurance specific exercises as a percentage of your OTW.

For exercises that concentrate on pure strength development, use 100 per cent of your OTW — that is, use the weight you can move eight times in an exercise. Perform six repetitions, pause to do a few minutes of stretching; perform another six repetitions,

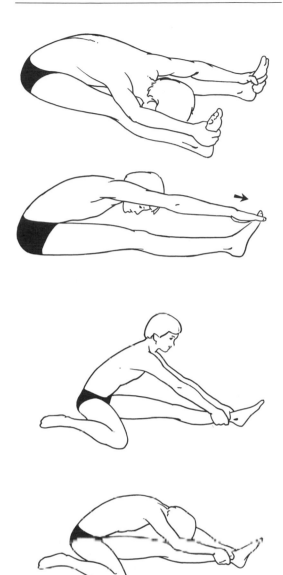

Unassisted basic knee, leg and hip stretching exercises. Keep legs straight and hold stretched position for 10–30 seconds.

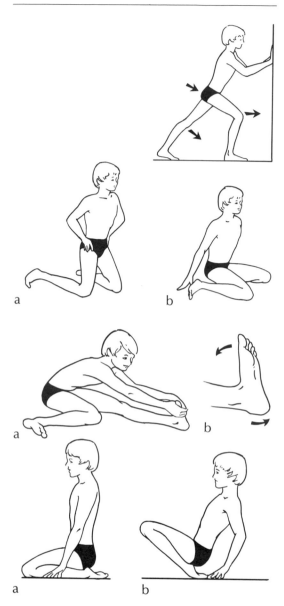

Unassisted ankle and knee stretching exercises. Hold stretched position for 10–30 seconds.

pause for more stretching; then perform a third set of six repetitions. When you can do the sixth repetition in the third set without effort, you are ready for a small weight increase.

For exercises that concentrate on developing endurance, use at first 50 per cent of your OTW—that is, use *half* the weight you can move eight times in an exercise. You want to develop the ability of the muscles to work over long periods of time without losing the quality of the performance. In swimming, almost all events are over one minute. This is a long time to have to put out a quality performance. Therefore, you must condition your muscles to support such a demand.

Perform 30 repetitions three times, with at least five minutes of stretching and relaxation between sets. When you can perform the third set easily, increase the weight to 55 per cent, then to 60 per cent of your OTW.

You should alternate strength development training and endurance development training weekly—that is, do strength one week and endurance the next. Do strength twice a week, on Tuesdays and Thursdays, for about 45 minutes, performing six different routines. Do endurance training three times a week, Monday, Wednesday and Friday, for about one hour, performing eight different routines.

Make sure you exercise both your upper and your lower body. It is recommended that 60 per cent of each session be spent on your upper body and 40 per cent on your lower body.

As you become good at the exercises, you can begin *carefully* to increase the speed that you do them at. This is more important for advanced swimmers, especially sprinters, than for novices.

In addition to weight training, there are other ways to develop your strength. One of the most recently developed pieces of equipment, specifically designed for swimming, is the biokinetic swim bench. Using this apparatus, you can closely reproduce the arm movements of the various strokes. You can do training sets for the same amount of time it takes to swim a race, and the machine will measure the effort you put out.

Points to remember about land training

- Stretching and calisthenics are a must, before you do any strenuous exercise, either in or out of the pool.
- Build up land training gradually, especially at the beginning of the season. Don't push yourself beyond the capabilities of your age and level of fitness.
- Move gradually from exercising your total body, to exercising specific parts of your body, in order to improve specific strokes and body motion. This is especially true in stretching and weight training.

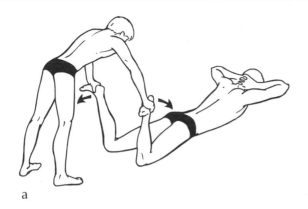

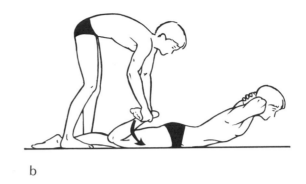

a

b

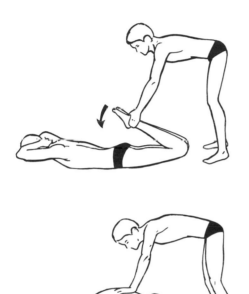

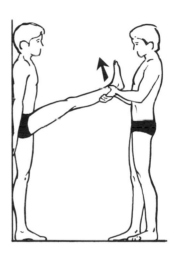

Basic ankle, knee, leg and hip stretching exercises. Keep legs perfectly straight when shown. In every case, hold stretched position for 10–30 seconds.

Some words from Alex

Our weight training consisted of about 12 to 15 exercises. During weightlifting sessions, I would concentrate on endurance rather than strength. Usually I did high repetitions with low weight. Other times I concentrated on low reps and high weight to increase strength. I still weight train but to a lesser extent than I used to.

When you do land training, it is easy to recognize the areas in which you are weak. Weight lifting helps you isolate the muscles you need to work on.

TRAINING THE MIND

The purpose of any training program is to develop the skills you need in order to swim well. You have learned about how to train your body, but you are more than just a body. Equally important is training your mind. Your body will put out its best effort only if your mind co-operates fully.

Your body is like the hardware of a computer and your mind is like the program or software. You can turn on the computer by plugging it in, just as you can make your body move by putting food into it. But you can't make a computer work for you unless you put in the program. In the same way, you can't make your body work for you unless you put your *mind* to it. There are certain ways to do this. Having a positive attitude, setting goals for yourself, committing yourself to your training and being willing to make sacrifices are all important states of mind for training.

Some words from Alex

Being in a good state of mind before a race is very important. This is especially true at the Olympics, where winning often comes down to the psychological element. After all, the eight finalists are probably equally capable physically.

Everyone is nervous before a race and this is completely normal. It is important to tune everything else out and focus solely on your race. Tell yourself that you are going out there to do your best and that is good enough. I usually prepare myself mentally by imagining the race in my mind beforehand. I concentrate on the split times for each stroke that my coach and I have set as goals.

A positive attitude
A specific attitude toward something, such as tackling a job or participating in a sport, is a state of mind that influences how you perform that job or sport. A positive attitude is obviously important if you are going to do well.

You are more likely to have a positive attitude toward swimming if your first contact with the swim club, the coach and the other athletes is friendly and comfortable. Don't be intimidated with stories of how difficult training is. You will not enjoy swimming, much less become skilled at it, if you don't like the atmosphere at the pool. It is important to like coming to the pool, to like the people, to like the games and the tasks you will need to perform.

If you have a positive attitude about these things, you will also have a positive attitude about equally important things, such as being on time for practice, paying attention to your coach and co-operating with your teammates. This in turn will lead you to become the best swimmer you can be.

Goal setting

In addition to developing a positive attitude, there are a few simple goals you should set for yourself. These will be different for the novice and for the advanced swimmer. If you are a novice, you need to focus more on your skills, while if you are a more advanced swimmer, you are ready to focus on performance.

Some words from Alex

As a novice swimmer, I set some short term goals for myself, such as perfecting a turn or swimming a part of a race faster than the other parts. During practice, I always tried to achieve a certain time on a particular set. It didn't matter whether this time was my very best, as long as I achieved that particular goal.

It is very important to set realistic goals, so that you can meet them and feel a sense of accomplishment. It is an important step in building your confidence.

Goals of the novice swimmer

- Never be satisfied that something is "good enough". Be a perfectionist.
- Begin with the simple skills and go on to the more difficult. You can't learn to swim in the deep end.
- Concentrate on performing each skill as nearly perfectly as you can, rather than as fast as you can. Speed will follow naturally from a stroke well done.
- Focus on the small tasks rather than worry about what is needed months down the road. Remember, many small goals achieved will eventually add up to excellence.

Some words from Alex

As I became an advanced swimmer, I changed my goals appropriately. When I achieved a goal, I would set a higher one, which brought me up to another level. Eventually, as the competition at the club became more limited for me, my own personal goals became much more important and I worked much harder on trying to beat my own world records and my own personal best.

Goals of the advanced swimmer

- Be concerned with day-to-day progress rather than instant success. Was the 1500-metre harder last week than today? How many 100-metre repeats were you able to keep under 1:05?
- Don't give up because a certain plan didn't work or a certain swim time wasn't accomplished. Be persistent. Find out the reasons it didn't work and try again.
- Be modest with intermediate goals. Think of improving your times little by little. Think of achieving times to qualify for

higher-calibre meets, rather than of winning and breaking records.

Commitment

Once you have set your goals and have them firmly in mind, you must *commit* yourself to accomplishing them.

- It is easier to accomplish your goals when they are small.
- Success in accomplishing your goals will build your confidence and strengthen your commitment to your program.
- Failure means you were not ready at the time. It does not mean you are not capable. With commitment, you will have the resolve to go back and try again.

Your commitment should increase as you progress in your program. But don't drop everything else from your life as a sign of total dedication. This is a false sense of commitment. Pursue your normal routine with other activities. When you are ready to prepare for a major international swimming event as a senior, then commitment will take on a different meaning.

Some words from Alex

To excel in any sport, you must make other sacrifices. For me, swimming has been the most important activity in my life. It has given me wonderful travelling experiences, friends around the world and an enormous sense of personal accomplishment. Because I spent so many hours in training and had to get up by 5:00 in the morning and go to bed at 9:30 in the evening, my time for other activities was very limited. I had to give up my social life, except for around the pool. It was often hard to keep up with my school work, especially when I travelled. But I managed by being super-organized.

If I had to do it all over again, I would make the same sacrifices. I feel that the benefits have far outweighed the sacrifices.

Sacrifice

In order to have commitment or dedication to your swimming program, it is sometimes necessary to *sacrifice* or give up certain activities at certain times. Deciding what to give up should be done with the help of your coach and parents. What you sacrifice should not be out of proportion with your goals and commitment.

- Don't give up recreational opportunities simply because you are an athlete. Decide whether or not the activity will interfere with your training.
- Always keep regular bedtime hours, even if it means missing a favourite TV program or having to leave a party early. This is

especially important during demanding training periods or just before a swim competition. If you keep irregular hours, your body will not function at its best.

- *Never* sacrifice school work, even if you are tempted to do so. Plan your daily schedule so that you can complete all your responsibilities and still find time for relaxing recreational activities.
- Give up junk food in favour of a strict, nutritious diet. It is easy to fall into poor eating habits, and junk food is often tempting, especially when you have a busy schedule. But with dedication, it can be just as easy to eat the right foods as the junk foods.

Points to remember about training the mind

- Training the mind involves having a positive attitude, setting goals for yourself, committing yourself to your training and being willing to make sacrifices.
- A good attitude cannot guarantee that you will succeed, but you cannot succeed without a good attitude.
- Focus on accomplishing small goals. Achieving many small goals will lead to the accomplishment of one large goal.
- Do not cut everything else out of your life as a sign of total dedication to your program. What you sacrifice should be in proportion to your goals and commitment.

TRAINING ON A TEAM

A team is a group of people who work together to achieve certain shared goals. You may have your own personal goals, but if you are part of a team, you will find that your *general* goal of achieving excellence is shared by the other team members. If you co-operate with the others and give each other support, everyone will achieve greater success than they could have on their own. When you accomplish team goals, it often inspires you and can lead you to personal success.

When you join a swim team, you join a group of people with a special way of life, a way of life that is organized so that there is time for all the important things: school, training, social activities, recreation, and rest and sleep. Of course, this doesn't mean you can do everything every day. Sometimes you will have to give up certain activities so that school and training can come first.

When you are part of a team, you will also have certain responsibilities. One of your responsibilities is to be dedicated to the goals of the team—particularly the goal of excellence. Many swim

The swim team Canada sent to the Olympic Summer Games in 1984.

ATHLETE INFORMATION BUREAU

teams have a booklet that lists the duties, training rules and codes of behaviour that each person must follow. You will find that it is easier to keep your responsibilities and to work hard for your goals, if you know other people are doing the same thing. This is what is meant by *team support*.

Swimming on a team has many advantages as well as responsibilities. Because you are working with others who share your interests, you will find that you develop close friendships with some of the other members, which sometimes last a lifetime. You will find that when things are tough, there will be friends nearby to help you and give you encouragement. This doesn't just apply to swimming. It could be a problem in school or at home. Because members of a swim team are not all the same age, you may also find there are older swimmers, with more experience both in life and in swimming, who can give you guidance. There will also be younger swimmers for whom you can be a resource.

It is important to remember that the team does not just consist of you and the other swimmers. The team also includes your coach or instructor and, in a sense, your parents. In order for the team to function at its best, there must be an open line of communication between you, your coach and your parents. This three-way relationship is called the *athletic triangle*.

Some words from Alex

Even though swimming is an individual sport, it is great to be part of a team. When I was growing up, my best friends were other team members at my club, because I had so much more in common with them. Teammates can provide you with special understanding and encouragement, since they are in the same situation as you.

At the Olympics, it was incredible to hear my teammates cheer when the announcer called my name before a race. When you know that the whole team is behind you, it inspires you and helps you perform better.

You and your parents

It is important that parents be kept informed about the team's goals, meets and functions. Swim teams rely on parents to fill officiating positions when the team is hosting a competition, to help plan recreational activities, and to organize fund raisers to raise money for the team.

It is part of a young swimmer's responsibilities to keep parents informed of his or her swimming progress. Success does not always mean winning the race. Success can be a well executed start or turn or breathing pattern. If a swimmer accomplishes one of these things, even if the race is lost, he or she will have accomplished a significant goal. If the youngster keeps his or her parents closely

The Athletic Triangle

informed of his or her progress, they too will be able to share in the accomplishments, and not be disappointed by the result of a race.

Parents should understand the training plan, so they understand why their youngster is practising certain skills in competitions, instead of trying to win. Young swimmers might even invite their parents occasionally to watch them train and see the skills that they are learning.

Some words from Alex

Being parents of a competitive swimmer is no easy task. It requires lots of co-operation, patience and understanding. My parents were always supportive of me in whatever I tried to accomplish. When I was young, they got up with me and drove me to the pool for training at ungodly early hours. They came to watch me at meets as often as they could. They never pushed me, but were always there when I needed them. My supportive home life was a vital factor in my swimming career.

The coach and parents

It is also important that the coach and parents get to know one another and meet regularly. Particularly when a swimmer is young, they can each help him or her be better if they are in communication with each other and know how the youngster is doing both at swim practices and at home.

Ideally, parents become involved with the team, and help officiate at local meets or serve as chaperons on out-of-town trips. This gives the coach a chance to meet parents more often and it gives them the opportunity to get to know each other. When parents and coach have a good meeting of minds, the swimmers are the ones who benefit the most.

You and your coach

Young swimmers may be accustomed to communicating and co-operating with their parents, but they have probably never worked with a swimming coach before. The coach is someone who has had a great deal of experience both in swimming and in training, and he or she will develop a plan that best helps the youngster to learn the skills he or she needs to know. The coach will go over with the student — and preferably write down — the goals of the program, the required team discipline, guidance for diet and rest, and other things he or she needs to know.

Any aspiring swimmer, but especially younger ones, should realize that the coach can only go so far in giving him the skills he needs. The youngster's co-operation and commitment are also necessary, if he or she is going to become a successful swimmer.

Young swimmers should realize that, like their parents and the other swimmers on the team, the coach is someone who cares about them, both in and out of the water. Often, personal problems can affect a swimmer's training, and the other way around. The young swimmer should be able to go to the coach with personal problems as well as problems with swimming.

If the swimmer, coach and parents are all working together as a team, he or she will find it easier to attend practices, do well in school work, improve swimming and enjoy recreation time. A properly working athletic triangle is essential for your training as a successful swimmer.

Some words from Alex

My coach, Dr. Tihanyi, has been crucial to my development both as a swimmer and as a person. He has been responsible for my swimming career, and it is without doubt that it was because of his program and his dedication to my career that I excelled in my sport. I don't think I could have won my medals without him.

Doc has also helped me in many personal ways to overcome the hurdles in my life, whether it was my shoulder injury or the deaths of my brother and my father. He was a parent figure to me and now he's one of my best friends.

SWIMMING AND YOUR BODY

A good training program is based on knowledge of how the systems of the body work together. Your body is made up of many *systems*. All the systems are interrelated. In other words, they work together to carry out your body's many functions. The systems most relevant to your swimming performance are the cardiovascular system (heart and blood vessels), respiratory system, digestive system and muscular system.

Training in sports is an organized process that makes the body's systems function more efficiently. In training, you exercise more and more intensely. Your body's systems adapt to the growing demands of training. This leads to greater strength and endurance, which leads to better swimming performance.

Some words from Alex

I have been told that I have a swimmer's body, but there is no particular body type that can guarantee success. Success comes from work and dedication.

Swimming can be a good sport to refine body systems and promote fitness, and it has a relatively low potential for injury. I believe swimming helped me to develop an efficient heart and lungs, and appreciate a good diet. My mother provided me with a balanced diet that not only helped me grow, but also gave me enough energy for my swimming. And the more I swam the stronger I became.

Energy and performance

What enables a swimmer to swim and train hard? The answer is *energy*. Energy is "the ability to do work". It also means "strength, force and power". Energy produced within your body makes your muscles and all the other parts of your body do work.

Energy comes from various sources. In a car, the source of energy is the fuel—usually gasoline. In your body, the source of energy is another type of fuel—food.

Food contains certain molecules, called *nutrients*, that your body needs in order to carry out its life processes. These life processes include breathing, moving, digesting, growth and repair, and so on. The two main nutrients that supply your body with energy are fats and carbohydrates. Examples of foods containing fats are milk, butter, ice cream, cheese and peanut butter. Examples of foods containing carbohydrates are bread, pasta, sugar, honey and potatoes.

When you eat foods, your stomach and intestines digest them. Your digestive system breaks most of the food down into nutrients. Complex chemical reactions take place so that your body's cells, including muscle cells, can absorb and use these nutrients in their work. When nutrients enter your body's cells, they help form an important energy-producing chemical called adenosine triphosphate, or ATP.

Besides food, your body's muscles also need oxygen in order to do work. Two systems in your body function together to supply oxygen to your muscles. These are the *respiratory system* and the *cardiovascular system*. Your lungs are part of your respiratory system. Your heart, veins, arteries and blood are part of your cardiovascular system.

When you inhale, oxygen from the air is deposited in tiny air sacs, called *alveoli*, in your lungs. The oxygen in the alveoli is collected by red blood cells travelling in tiny blood vessels called *capillaries*. The red blood cells contain a special form of the mineral iron, called *haemoglobin*. Haemoglobin carries the oxygen to your muscles. There it is used, along with food, as fuel to generate energy. At the same time, the alveoli pick up carbon dioxide — the waste product of your muscles' work — from the blood in the capillaries. You exhale this carbon dioxide.

This description of respiration is oversimplified. But it helps explain why certain dietary habits are recommended for swimmers. Eating a wide range of healthy foods, as well as foods known to be rich in iron, will help maintain high levels of haemoglobin in your blood. The more haemoglobin in your blood, the more oxygen can be carried to your muscles. The more oxygen carried to your muscles, the more efficiently they will work. Many other factors, of course, affect how much oxygen your blood can carry. However, eating a well-balanced, iron-rich diet is one way to increase your blood's oxygen-carrying capacity.

Blood transports oxygen from your lungs to your muscles. There are two different networks of blood vessels. One network — the arteries and the capillaries — carries the blood to your muscles. Another network — the veins — carries blood containing waste products away from the muscles.

Exercising your heart

Your heart pumps the blood throughout your body. When a muscle is made to work, it usually enlarges. This is true of your heart. The more the heart is made to work during training, the larger and stronger it will become. A larger, stronger heart can pump more blood, and therefore more oxygen, to the working muscles. During exercise, a well-trained heart can deliver five to seven times more blood than when the body is at rest.

Your heart pumps blood and oxygen to your muscles. When you are swimming or doing aerobic exercises, you need extra blood and oxygen pumped to your muscles to keep you going. You have probably noticed that at the beginning of the training season, or when you are out of shape, you become short of breath more easily and your heart thumps harder during workouts. The reason your heart speeds up is that it is trying to pump more blood and oxygen to your muscles. As you become more fit, you will notice your heart doesn't have to work as hard when you swim or run. This is because you have trained your heart, through repeated exercise, to deliver the extra blood and oxygen you need.

It is important to keep track of the rate of your heart beat throughout your training, in addition to keeping track of your swim times and the number of lengths you do in a workout. This is another way of measuring your progress. To keep track of how fast your heart is beating, you determine what is called the *minute heart rate*. This is the number of times your heart beats in a minute. As you become more fit (as your swim times get shorter and as the distances you swim become longer), you will find the minute heart rate will become a smaller number. But your heart is actually pumping more blood. Through exercise, you have made it more efficient.

The number of times that your heart beats per minute when you are sitting or lying still is your *resting heart rate*. When you begin to exercise, your heart beat will quickly increase from the resting rate. The amount it increases depends on how strenuous the exercise is (the harder you work, the harder your heart works). When the heart rate has increased to the maximum amount it needs to for the work you are doing, it has reached the *steady state*. It keeps this number of beats until you slow down or stop. When you stop, your heart gradually returns to resting rate. How fast it returns to resting rate, how fast you *recover*, depends on how fit you are. The more fit you are, the faster it returns to resting rate. This is called the *recovery rate*.

How to measure your heart rate

The most accurate way to measure your heart rate is by using a special machine. It is not likely you will have access to this kind of machine, but it is possible for you to measure your heart rate simply by putting your fingers over your pulse and counting. This may not be as accurate a method as when a machine is used, but through practice, you can become quite skilled. In any case, it will give you an idea of your progress.

To find your pulse (heart beat), place one or two fingers on your neck to the left or right of your Adam's apple, or on the inside of your wrist on the thumb side, just above the wrist bone. You can also place your hand above your heart on your chest, although it is harder to get a pulse here, unless your heart is pounding very hard.

As soon as you have stopped the exercise you have been doing (at least within five seconds), find your pulse and count your heart beats for ten seconds. Multiply this number by six (10 seconds × 6 = 60 seconds or 1 minute), and you will get your *minute heart rate*.

It is not a good idea to compare your heart rate with that of other swimmers, because everyone's heart rate is different. Also, the younger you are, the higher your resting heart rate, and girls tend to have higher heart rates than boys. Your coach should be able to help you determine what your heart rate should be after different swimming events, and how high your heart rate should be during different forms of training.

Points to remember about swimming and your body

- Make a habit of counting your heart rate after important swim sets so you can associate heart rates with times. This way you will learn to evaluate how hard you work.
- Help your body systems work harmoniously by maintaining a proper balance between your training, rest and diet.
- Keep a diary of your heart rate to follow how your body is coping with training. Record your wake-up (basal) heart rate, your resting heart rate and the different training heart rates you achieve.
- Discuss the different heart rate values with your coach to better understand their meaning.

SWIMMING AND NUTRITION

In the previous sections, you have learned about how you must train your body and your mind to become the best swimmer you can be. But you can't put out your best effort if you don't eat the proper quantity of good, nutritious food. It is like preparing a car for a race. You can do all the necessary mechanical things to get the car into good running order, but it won't go anywhere if you don't put in gas. Just as you have to put good quality gas in the car, so you have to put good quality food inside you.

In order for your body to function at peak condition, you have to make sure you are taking in *nutrients*. There are six nutrient groups: vitamins, minerals, carbohydrates, protein, fat and water. You need all of these to make your body run efficiently.

Vitamins are necessary for the growth, vitality and general well-being of your body. They are found in milk, meat, dark green leafy and yellow vegetables, root vegetables such as potatoes and carrots, and fruits.

Minerals are important for body maintenance and cell building. Examples of common minerals are calcium, potassium, magnesium, iron and zinc. They are found in almost all foods, but especially in milk, fruits, vegetables and grains.

Carbohydrates are the best source of energy for athletes. There are two kinds of carbohydrates: simple and complex. Simple carbohydrates include sugar, fruit, honey, cookies, cakes and other foods containing sugar. Complex carbohydrates are found in breads, buns, bagels, spaghetti, macaroni and other noodles, potatoes, peas, carrots and baked beans. During training, you should make sure you are eating a wide variety of carbohydrates, especially the complex kind, which are the most nutritious source of energy. Sixty to 70 per cent of your diet should be carbohydrates.

Protein is another source of energy, but only if the energy is not being provided by carbohydrates or fats. Generally, protein builds and repairs body cells in the skin, blood, muscles, etc. Good sources of protein are meat, fish, poultry, milk, cheese, eggs, vegetables, beans and grain. Twelve to 18 per cent of the food you eat should be in the form of protein.

Fat has become somewhat of a taboo food, but there are good kinds of fat as well as bad. The bad fats are *saturated* fats, found in meat, egg yolk, milk, butter, cream and cheese, as well as many desserts. This doesn't mean you shouldn't eat these foods, but you should be careful not to overeat them. The good fats are *unsaturated* fats, found in vegetable oils derived from corn, soybean, olive oil and safflower. No more than 20 per cent of your diet should be fat.

Since most of our body is composed of water, it is important that you consume a lot. *Water* is found in the foods we eat — particularly fruits and vegetables — as well as in the liquids we

2500 (approximate) Calorie Plan

Time	Food	Calories
Pre-training Breakfast	125 mL orange juice 250 mL low-fat yogurt 1 banana	40 125 100
Post-training Breakfast	500 mL cereal 250 mL low-fat (2%) milk 1 apple 4 Graham crackers	210 125 60 110
Lunch	hamburger or turkey breast 1 bun 500 mL vegetable salad, no dressing 250 mL low-fat (2%) milk 8 Graham crackers	300 80 100 125 220
Pre-training Afternoon snack	2 slices whole wheat toast 125 mL apple sauce 250 mL low-fat (2%) milk	200 40 125
Dinner	250 mL beans in *burrito* 500–750 mL raw vegetables 250 mL low-fat (2%) milk	230 75 125
Before bed	1.5 L plain popcorn 125 mL tomato juice	180 40

drink. Fresh, cool tap water is the best source of water. It is important to drink lots of water during training and competition, especially when it is hot.

Some words from Alex

It is very important to eat a balanced diet. Food is the fuel for your body and serious swimming requires even more fuel than normal, everyday activity.

I was very fortunate to have a mother who cooked balanced meals from the basic food groups. When I was in training, I always tried to eat a lot of carbohydrates, such as potatoes and spaghetti, to give me the energy I needed for my rigorous training. I consumed between 6000 and 8000 calories a day when I was in intense training.

3000 (approximate) Calorie High-carbohydrate Plan

Time	Food	Calories
Pre-training Breakfast	250 mL juice	110
	3 slices whole wheat toast with butter/margarine	255
	15 mL jam	60
Post-training Breakfast	250 mL low-fat (2%) milk	125
	250 mL cereal	140
	2 apples or 500 mL juice	120
	4 Graham crackers	110
Lunch	250 mL skim milk	85
	Tossed salad, no dressing	100
	2 slices bread with 85 g fish/poultry	200
	5 mL butter/margarine	45
	250 mL fruit salad (fresh if possible)	80
Pre-training snack	1 banana	100
	250 mL juice	80
Dinner	250 mL skim milk	85
	250–500 mL cooked vegetables	75
	Tossed salad, no dressing	100
	625 mL potato/rice/pasta	350
	5 mL butter/margarine	45
	85 g meat/fish/poultry	100
	Fresh or canned fruit	100
Before bed	500 mL juice	220
	4 Graham crackers	110

Preparing a meal plan

There are complicated ways to determine how much of each nutrient you are consuming. The easiest way to make sure you are getting proper nutrition is to follow the *Canada Food Guide*. You may have learned about this guide in school. It divides everything we eat into four groups: (1) milk, (2) meat and poultry, (3) breads and (4) fruits and vegetables. The *Guide* recommends that you eat from each group at every meal. If you do this, you will be eating a healthy, nutritious diet.

In addition to following the *Canada Food Guide*, as a swimmer in training you need to make sure you are eating enough food to give you the extra energy you need to train. You might ask your-

4000 (approximate) Calorie Plan

Time	Food	Calories
Pre-training Breakfast	3 slices whole wheat toast with butter/margarine	300
	250 mL orange juice	110
	250 mL skim milk	85
Post-training Breakfast	2 boiled eggs	160
	250 mL bran flakes	105
	250 mL skim milk	85
	3 slices whole wheat toast with butter/margarine	300
	250 mL grapefruit juice	95
Lunch	2 tuna sandwiches on whole wheat bread	450
	250 mL skim milk	85
	250 mL orange juice	110
	8 Graham crackers	220
	Raw vegetables	75
Pre-training snack	1 banana	100
	8 Graham crackers	220
	250 mL skim milk	85
Dinner	140 g baked chicken breast (no skin)	150
	500 mL mashed potatoes with skim milk	300
	250 mL cooked lima beans	170
	125 mL cooked beets	26
	Large salad with low-calorie dressing	150
	250 mL skim milk	85
Before bed	1.5 L plain popcorn	180
	375 mL grapefruit juice	142
	125 mL plain yogurt	100

self, what makes cars go? Gasoline, of course. What about flashlights and watches? Probably an alkaline battery. Both the gasoline and the battery are sources of energy. What makes you swim and train hard? Energy, which comes from food sources stored in the body. Obviously someone who swims every day needs more energy than someone who leads a less active life. And obviously the longer and harder you train, the more energy you need.

Energy is measured in *calories*. Each item of food you eat has a certain number of calories in it. If you add up all the calories of everything you eat all day, you will get your *daily caloric intake*. The harder you train and the more energy you need, the more calories you need to take in. You may hear your coach speak of the *caloric requirements* for certain training programs. This means that to have the energy to do a certain program, you'll need to take in a certain number of calories each day. But there are calories from bad sources of food as well as good sources. It is important to get your calories from healthy sources (such as those listed in the *Canada Food Guide*). It is also important that you consume more than 50 per cent of your caloric intake by the end of lunch.

Here are some daily meal plans for three different caloric intakes: 2500 calories, 3000 calories and 4000 calories. These menus are carefully planned to give you all the nutrients you need each day. For each plan, there are both pre-training and post-training meals.

To train effectively, you should always eat some food, but not too much, before training. This meal is referred to as the pre-training meal. But your big meal should always follow your training. Never neglect it, because your post-training meal will replenish all the energy that you used up during training.

You can make up your own meal plans by following the *Canada Food Guide* and buying or borrowing from the library a reference book that lists the calories in each food. This often comes in pocket size and is called a "Calorie Counter".

Eating on the day of the meet

If you know what to eat, when to eat and how much to eat on the day of the meet, chances are you will swim better. Here are some easy-to-follow tips:

- Eat a light meal, containing no more than about 450 calories, three to four hours before competing. This will make sure your stomach and upper intestine are empty.
- Make sure to include carbohydrates such as whole grain breads, buns, bagels, pasta, potatoes and/or carrots in your meals. These are the best sources of energy.
- Drink lots of cool water, about one glass every quarter to half hour.
- If you drink juice or sports drinks, dilute them with water or drink cool water afterwards to dilute them in your stomach.
- Eat small amounts of food (about 250 to 350 calories) regularly during the day.
- Avoid greasy foods, such as french fries or any fried foods, as they take a long time to digest.
- Plan what you are going to eat on the day of a competition ahead of time. Try eating these foods on certain training days. If the plan works for you, use it for every competition.

Some words from Alex

On the day of a competition, I always had an early big breakfast, including eggs, potatoes and toast. After the morning heats, I had a big lunch — something like spaghetti or chicken. I would then rest and try to grab a snack, an apple or granola bar, an hour before the finals. At night after the finals, I usually ate a big meal and a salad.

Points to remember about nutrition

- Food is a source of *energy*. Energy makes your body function.
- Proper nutrition will ensure that your body functions at top capacity.
- If you follow the *Canada Food Guide* and keep track of your daily caloric intake, you will be sure to get the right nutrients and the right amount of food.

EQUIPMENT AND TRAINING AIDS

Training aids and proper equipment are a necessary part of any swim program. They are important because they can help you improve your stroke technique and add variety to your training. There are three different types of equipment that you will use: personal equipment, pool equipment and training equipment. It would take too long to describe *all* the equipment that comes under these categories, so below you will find descriptions only of the equipment that it is *necessary* for you to have.

Some words from Alex

My favourite training aids are the biokinetic swim bench and surgical tubing. Surgical tubing is like a tethered swim. You tie it around your waist and secure the other end around a starting block. As you swim, there is more and more resistance, until you are hardly moving by the end of the length. This is good for your strength and technique in the pool.

Personal equipment

Make sure that all your personal equipment is in the club colours. If you and your teammates all have the same colours, you will feel you really belong to a team.

Nylon training suit

Bathing suits made of nylon are sturdier and will hold up better under constant use in chlorinated water than suits made of other materials. Swimmers usually wear several swim suits on top of one another during training so they have more resistance, allowing a better workout. Old, worn-out suits are good for wearing under the good nylon suit. Buy your training suit a size or two too large. It should fit loosely, and you should be able to wear the other suits underneath it. When you put on your competitive suit it should feel light, so you can move easily and fast.

Lycra competitive suit

Lycra suits are made of stretchy material to fit you snugly. This suit should be at least two sizes smaller than your nylon suit. Don't worry if it feels uncomfortable at first. It should feel small and very snug. Rinse your Lycra suit in cold fresh water after each use, to slow down the deterioration caused by the chlorine.

Goggles

Goggles come in so many shapes and sizes that there will be a pair to fit you, no matter what shape or size your face is. The use of goggles changed training drastically, because they protect your eyes so you can stay in the water longer. You can also see other swimmers under water and learn from watching how they do their strokes. You should make sure your goggles fit well so they won't leak and will stay on your face during dive starts.

> **Some words from Alex**
>
> *Goggles have always been essential equipment for me. They must fit well and comfortably. Take your time in choosing the right ones for you. Make sure your equipment is in satisfactory condition because the last thing you want is a surprise, like broken goggles, just before you are ready to compete.*

Swim cap

You should wear a swim cap both to protect your hair from pool chemicals and to keep it out of your face. However, because swim caps are made of rubber latex, which can make you feel quite hot, you may not want to wear one in a longer event competition. To help your cap last longer, rinse it in fresh cold water, dry it and sprinkle it with baby powder after each use.

Pool equipment

Lane dividers

For training, you may use the less expensive ropes that have a float about every half metre. The problem with these kinds of ropes, however, is that they offer no wave control. This means that if there are large numbers of swimmers in the pool, the water may be very rough. When you are swimming in rough water, you will sometimes concentrate more on plowing through the waves, than on doing your strokes accurately.

There are lane ropes that keep the water calm. They are not actually "ropes" but a series of plastic disks designed to cut down on the wave activity. These more expensive dividers should definitely be used in competitions. Ideally, they should be used all the time. If this isn't possible, they should at least be used for sessions in which you are concentrating on stroke skills.

Starting blocks

Starting blocks are used in a competition, but you will also need to use them to practise your diving starts during training sessions. The top platform of the block should be large enough to allow you to grip the front edge for the grab start. It is important that these blocks be equipped with hand grips for the backstroke start.

Backstroke turn flags

These flags should be multi-coloured and easy to see. They should be suspended over the water five metres from each end wall of the pool, so that when you are doing the backstroke you will know when you are coming to the end of the pool. It is very important that these flags always be in place during training.

Pace clocks

Swimming against the clock is the most common way to prepare for competition. You should become accustomed to using a pace clock right from the start of your swimming career. A training pace clock should be placed at each end of the pool and others half way along the pool sides where you can see them from the water. The clock will help you to control the pace and speed of your lengths. With the clock, your coach won't always have to be timing you, but can focus on your strokes.

Some words from Alex

Swimming with a pace clock has always been fun for me. I often played games with the clock — like trying to make better times from set to set. The clock can make you very competitive, especially if you set time goals for yourself. I sometimes tried to predict my time while I was coming into the wall. By the time I was 18, I didn't have much competition at the club, so I often raced against the clock.

Training equipment

Some training equipment provides support, while other equipment provides extra resistance to help you increase your strength and endurance.

Some words from Alex

I enjoy using training equipment such as hand paddles, kickboards and fins in swimming practice. They add variety to my workouts and help me to isolate different muscles I want to work on. Flippers were especially helpful to me in learning the dolphin movement in the butterfly stroke.

Kickboard

Use a kickboard when you want to practise your butterfly, breast or freestyle kick. Hold the board at arm's length with your hands gripping the top, so that your shoulders are low or close to the level of the water. If you want to make your legs work even harder, use two or three boards piled on top of each other. Make sure you are holding the board properly or you might find you're not using the right kicking technique. Spend time kicking both with and without the board.

Diving fins

Kicking with fins will help you learn the correct technique for the freestyle, backstroke and butterfly kicks. Fins make the kick much easier to do and you will be able to feel what it should be like. The use of fins will also increase the flexibility of your ankles. When you use fins during timed swims, you will feel much better about your times because your kick will be so much faster and more powerful! It is good to vary the water resistance.

Hand paddles

Hand paddles come in many different sizes and designs, so there will always be one kind to fit you. Hand paddles help you improve your stroke technique, and like the kick fins, they will give you a feel for the way the stroke should be done.

When you are just beginning training, you should use paddles for technique work only. When you are more experienced, you can use the smaller paddles for technique and sprinting, and the larger paddles for overload work—that is, to provide more water resistance so you work harder. There are finger paddles that can be used for the breaststroke and forearm paddles for learning the use of the inner surface of the whole arm. With these paddles, you do not use your hands. Therefore when you swim without them, your whole arm may feel like your paddling hand.

Flotation and drag devices

Flotation devices are sometimes attached to your legs or ankles to keep your legs afloat, while your arms do all the work. (They are the opposite of the kickboard, which keeps your upper body afloat while your legs do all the work.) Drag devices are like flotation devices, except that they are bigger or heavier and therefore make your upper body work harder. (This is like piling up two or three kickboards to make your legs work harder.)

Pull buoys are the simplest of the devices. They come in different sizes and are placed between the ankles or knees or between the upper part of the thighs. Pull buoys can be used in combination with *inner tube strips* or with *tire tubes*, which are both placed around the ankles. Both the inner tube strips and the tire tubes will create additional drag.

Be careful how you use training equipment. During the early part of the season, you should not use training equipment. You should only begin to use it after you are in good physical shape. Also be careful not to misuse or overuse training aids, as this can cause injury. For example, overuse of fins may cause problems in the ankle joints. Too much paddle work and tube work may cause problems in the shoulders. But proper use of training aids can help you improve your skills and your strength.

Points to remember about equipment and training aids

- Wear several *nylon* suits for training and a snug fitting *Lycra* suit for competitions.
- Always rinse out your suit in fresh cold water after wearing, to slow down deterioration from chlorine.
- Be sure backstroke flags are always in place during training sessions.
- Do not overuse or misuse training aids, or you may cause injury. Proper use can help you improve your skills and strength.

PERSONAL DATA RECORD

The height and weight of swimmers in training, especially of those between the ages of 10 and 17 years, should be recorded on a weekly basis. The percentage of body fat should, if possible, be calculated once a month.

The body fat calculation gives both coach and swimmer an indication of how much muscle and bone the swimmer has. Generally speaking, for boys, body fat should be below 14 per cent, and for girls, below 20 per cent.

Body fat calculations can usually be obtained from sports medicine clinics or university sports science departments.

YEAR	MONTH	DAY	HEIGHT (cm)	WEIGHT (kg)	% BODY FAT

DAILY TRAINING LOG

It is important to keep a record of what is accomplished in each training session: the stroke that is practised, the drills learned, the distance kicked, pulled and swum.

The log also provides space in which to comment on the session. Were the distances too long? In which areas are more drills needed? Which skills are weak and which strong?

Note that SC and LC are abbreviations for "short course" (25 metres) and "long course" (50 metres) respectively.

DATE

A.M.	TIME: _____	SC ☐ (25 m course)	HEART RATE AT WAKE UP: _____
		LC ☐ (50 m course)	

COMMENTS:

TOTAL DRILL: _____
TOTAL KICK: _____
TOTAL PULL: _____
TOTAL SWIM: _____
TOTAL METRES: _____

P.M.	TIME: _____	SC ☐
		LC ☐

COMMENTS:

TOTAL DRILL: _____
TOTAL KICK: _____
TOTAL PULL: _____
TOTAL SWIM: _____
TOTAL METRES: _____

CUMULATIVE MONTHLY TRAINING DISTANCES

Maintaining an accurate monthly record makes it easier to analyze the swimmer's progress in the training program as a whole. Have some skills been over-emphasized and others neglected? A review of the monthly totals should allow coach and swimmer to explain weak skills and to refocus their approach.

Swim meets and time trials should also be recorded on the appropriate lines.

MONTH:

DAY	SWIM A.M.	SWIM P.M.	PULL A.M.	PULL P.M.	KICK A.M.	KICK P.M.	DRILL A.M.	DRILL P.M.	TOTAL METRES FOR DAY	LAND TRAINING
1										
2										
3										
4										
5										
6										
7										
8										
9										
10										
11										
12										
13										
14										
15										
16										
17										
18										
19										
20										
21										
22										
23										
24										
25										
26										
27										
28										
29										
30										
31										
MONTH TOTALS										

PERSONAL COMPETITION SPLIT TIME RECORDS

By maintaining a record of the "splits" — the times attained by the swimmer over different segments of the course — the coach and swimmer can identify weak aspects of the races and refocus the training program accordingly.

MEET AND LOCATION:								DATE	SC	LC	HEAT	FINAL
WARM UP DISTANCE:												
DIST. →										TOTAL TIME		PLACE
EVENT	SPLIT	SPLIT	SPLIT	SPLIT	SPLIT	SPLIT	SPLIT	SPLIT				
COMMENTS:												

MEET AND LOCATION:								DATE	SC	LC	HEAT	FINAL
WARM UP DISTANCE:												
DIST. →										TOTAL TIME		PLACE
EVENT	SPLIT	SPLIT	SPLIT	SPLIT	SPLIT	SPLIT	SPLIT	SPLIT				
COMMENTS:												

MEET AND LOCATION:								DATE	SC	LC	HEAT	FINAL
WARM UP DISTANCE:												
DIST. →										TOTAL TIME		PLACE
EVENT	SPLIT	SPLIT	SPLIT	SPLIT	SPLIT	SPLIT	SPLIT	SPLIT				
COMMENTS:												

PERSONAL TIME RECORDS

As they become faster, most swimmers find satisfaction in keeping a record of their racing times. Remember, however, especially in the early years of training, that improving skills is more important than improving times.

EVENT / DATE / MEET	SC M	LC Yds.	SC M	LC Yds.	SC M	LC Yds.	SC M	LC Yds.	SC M	LC Yds.	SC M	LC Yds.	SC M	LC Yds.	SC M	LC Yds.	SC M	LC Yds.	SC M	LC Yds.	SC M	LC Yds.
Free 50																						
100																						
200																						
400 / 500																						
800 / 1500																						
Back 50																						
100																						
200																						
Breast 50																						
100																						
200																						
Fly 50																						
100																						
200																						
IM 100																						
200																						
400																						

SWIMMING WITH ALEX BAUMANN

A PROGRAM FOR COMPETITIVE AND RECREATIONAL SWIMMERS